Odd One Out

Radical Revelations

on Relationships, Self-Help,

and Personal Growth

By

JOHN LEE

Odd One Out

RADICAL REVELATIONS ON RELATIONSHIPS,
SELF-HELP, AND PERSONAL GROWTH

JOHN LEE

Teitelbaum Publishing

ISBN: 978-1-7363675-2-0

Dedicated

To my old friend and fellow outsider

Caleb Curren

JOHN LEE

ACKNOWLEDGMENTS

If I was a talented enough poet, I'd write each of the people a personal love sonnet, but I'm not so I'll just say it like it is. I'd thank Robert Bly for deliberate friendship and mentorship, Bill Stott for always being there for me and contributing to my well-being, Susan Lee for continuity and caring, Kathy Lee McClelland for always believing in me and cheering me on, Robert and Carol Teitlebaum for their kindness and support of my work by publishing my recent books, Pat Love for listening to me and making me laugh for years, Lindsey Lane who always tells me the truth, and finally, my mother and father who have done their best trying to understand and keep loving their strange, outsider son.

PREFACE

I was born in 1951 In Detroit, Michigan to rural, southern, Appalachian parents who loaded up the truck and
moved to Motor City to find work that paid much better than
share-cropping and farming. There I didn't fit in with the
native urbanites. I developed a strong "yankee" accent and
then at nine years old my folks, my uncles, aunts and cousins
all moved back down South — well let's just say supreme
culture shock. When I got to Crossville, Alabama, again I was
a quintessential outsider who was picked on, made fun of and
bullied by the kids in school, but even from a few uncles who
never left their farm or chicken houses. My Northern tongue
became the bane of my existence by people who were still
reminiscing about the war between the states.

As fast as possible I began to learn to speak Southern redneck, which if you have heard my lectures or talks, you know
I have mastered. Even in my family I was the black sheep and
still am the outsider and not very much like other members of
my extended family but who I love dearly and who loves me
in spite of my eccentricities and idiosyncratic views on life.

Now at the almost tender young age of 70 and still the
outsider I am going to ask you, the reader, to think differently
about a whole host of things we've been taught or told about
psychology, relationships, therapy, anger, men's issues, love,
poetry and much more no matter what part of the country you
are from.

J.L.

JOHN LEE

CONTENTS

Part 1. Thinking About Things Differently

Are We Afraid or Anxious?

Eros and Thanatos: Passion and Death

Caring for Someone or Caretaking

Designated Problem: Let's Get Rid of It

Closure: A Made-up Relationship Term

Why We Can't be Rejected

The Illusion and Reality of Abandonment

Are You Empathetic or Sympathetic?

Feeling Guilty: Maybe Not

They Love You in Their Own Way

Are You Feeling Melancholy?

Regression: The Damage

Honesty: Brutal or Rigorous

Boundaries

The Differences Between Depression and Despair

Identifying Passivity

Symptoms of Depression and Passivity

Solving the Problem of Passivity

Every Time You Say "You" You Will Pay

How to Tell the Difference Between Anger and Rage

Interruption Rage: The Kind of Rage No One Has Talked About

Solving the Anger Problem for Alcoholics, Addicts and

Those Who Love Us

Anger as Punishment and Revenge

Fair Fighting: Seven Steps

Surrendering to What Is: Staying Open to What Will Be

Insane for the Light

"Why?" The Most Useless Question

Unbecoming: From Despair to Love

I'm Not Your Mother and I'm Not Your Father: How We Speak to Adults

Feelings Are as Important as Facts

Letting Your Feelings Out of the Cage

Isn't It Touching?

So, What's the Holdup on Being Held?

I Lost Myself

The Loneliness Emergency: From Isolation to Connection

Masculinity

Home for the Holidays

Grieving: The Doorway to Healing and Maturity

Third Act of Life

Seven Years to Seven Minutes

What Now?

And Now a Break from Psychology and Into the Realm of Fairytales

Part 2. Reflections from My Previous Published Works

Writing from the Body: For Writers, Artists, and Dreamers
Who Long to Free Their Voice

The Flying Boy: Healing the Wounded Man

The Flying Boy Letters: Getting Back to Y'all 30 Years
Later

  Roller Coaster Rider

  I'm Over-Anxious Joan

  Who Never Felt So Hopeless and Lost

  I Can't Get Angry at My Mother

Courting a Woman's Soul

  In Search of the Feminine

  Courting the Souls of the Ones You Love: The Platinum
  Rule of Loving

Where Do I Go from Her?

A Quiet Strength: Meditations on the Masculine Soul

  Making Peace

  Returning the Earth

  Earth, the Great Teacher

  A Wordless Language

  The Language of Animals

  The True Work

  Deep Respect

  Fire

  Youth and the Flying Boy

  Where is the Treasure?

  Conflict

JOHN LEE

Part 3. Personal Stories

   Life Is a Funny Old Dog
   Machine Shop
   Pagans, Poetry, and Preachers
   School-Dazed and Confused

Part 4. Poetry

   Some Marriages
   Noisy Silence
   Thunderstorm in Mentone
   Holding On
   Ancient Paths
   The Long Walk Home

INTRODUCTION

I needed the money to supplement the poverty wages I was making as a teaching assistant while working on my master's degree at the University of Alabama in Tuscaloosa. I took a job as a counselor/babysitter at what the State called a Center for "emotionally disturbed children" – a euphemism for a holding tank for boys and girls who had been beaten, abused, molested, and generally abandoned by parents that were more emotionally disturbed than their children.

I was 28 and had become seriously interested in Humanistic Psychology, with a subscription to the *Journal* and everything. I'd been reading Carl Rogers, Abraham Maslow, Fritz Perls, and other giants in the field. There was little that was humanistic or vaguely humane about the Center. Behavior Modification was all the rage and was a major contributor to much of the children's rage – their abuse notwithstanding. The pinning down on the floor or against the wall of a kid who was "acting out" and/or hurting themselves or others, was S.O.P. The Time-Out room was the method du jour of choice if the pinning or withdrawal of privileges did not work. The cold cement, steel reinforced door, ugly yellow painted walls, and equally ugly linoleum floor – yeah, that was exactly what those kids needed after being hardened and frozen to death from lack of affection, slaps in the face, or in the case of Genene, hammered on the nose by her father

until it sat sideways on her face. Even the social workers and
nursing staff was quick to grab an offender and push, shove,
drag or throw them into the tiny concrete box.

I remember thinking that if I ever started resorting to
the Time-Out room as a first resort because of impatience,
inhumanness, or thoughtlessness that I would quit and flip
burgers to make my tuition.

At staff meetings each week the so-called treatment team
– or perhaps I should say, mistreatment team – would meet
and review each "case" and evaluate the progress, or more
often, the lack of progress, convinced their subjects were
just resistant to their therapeutic techniques and modalities
– Psychologists, "More time outs are necessary." Social
Worker, "No, we need to make the points more difficult to
obtain." Psychiatrist, "No, higher doses of medication."
Nurse, "No, we need to change their medication." Lead
counselor, "So do we all agree?" would ask as she looked at
the eight or ten of us sitting in the jury box – I mean, at the
conference table.

"Not me," was my usual response. This standard objection
over the twelve months I was there got to be a running joke
with her and the other therapists. They pretty much agreed
after hearing my alternative approaches that I was idealistic
and naïve to proceed as if they were people instead of
projects, pets, or problems.

One such problem in their eyes was J. T., a shiny, nine-year-old black boy that was just the kind of case that Behavior Mod was designed for. The wiry, funny kid kept wetting his bed each and every night. "So, do we all agree that the electric shock pad is the way to go, except for you John?" said the psychiatrist with a slight note of sarcasm in his voice. Right, there was one of the main reasons I couldn't finish my bachelor's in psychology because I couldn't work up the nerve, or downgrade what little consciousness I had, and attach electrodes to un-emotionally disturbed mice and make them maniacs in a cage. "Here's what I'd like to do. I want to take J. T. home with me in the evenings for one week and see if my methods will help him stop his bed wetting." The staff agreed, much to my surprise, and I'm sure it was because it meant one less headache each night and morning.

J. T. was glad to get out of the chaos to be sure. When we got to my house that first evening, I sat J. T. down, "So here's what we're going to do," pointing to the guest bedroom. "That will be your room and you will have the mattress lying on the floor." Before I could finish my sentence, he folded his arms over his wiry chest, stuck out his bottom lip and said, "I don't want to sleep on the bed. I'll just sleep on the floor." He spoke really fast for a southerner as if the speed of his protest would ease the embarrassment.

"Is that because of the peeing thing?" I asked.

"I don't pee," he fired back.

"Yes, you do, and you know what, it doesn't bother me a bit."

"Why not?" He seemed really curious since no one at the Center held that point of view.

"Because it won't be me sleeping in the bed and it won't be me carrying it outside every morning – that will be you. If you wet the bed, then each morning you can drag the mattress outside and put it on the picnic table to dry and air out."

Long story short, he urinated on it the first three nights he spent with me. Every morning he grumbled and complained about how heavy it was. By the fourth, fifth, sixth, and seventh night it was dry as a bone and he slept as sound as a bear in wintertime.

J. T. had to return to the Center at the end of the seven days. One week was all they were willing to risk having the boy stay with the weird, humanistic, pseudo-Jungian counselor with long hair and a beard, and who bad-mouthed Behavior Mod. After all, they were sure the three nights he didn't wet the bed was just a "coincidence."

The first night back the bed was soaked. The next morning everyone agreed the shock pad was really the right way to go – well everyone except J. T. and me.

But the straw that broke this college student's back was after working there for a while fighting off B.F. Skinner's disciples and getting frustrated with Pavlov's children, I found myself doing the unthinkable only months before. Genene was acting out and I dragged her kicking, screaming, and sobbing into the Time-Out room without so much as a humanistic thought in my head or heart. She pushed with all her might against the door I was trying so desperately to close on her.

"Please, please, I'm begging you, don't leave me alone in here. I'll be good. I'll do anything. Please, please, please don't shut the door," she screamed at the top of her lungs as snot ran out of her bent, crooked nose. I finally mustered up enough strength to wrestle her in, shut the door, and walk down the hall. Even through the closed door and a hundred feet away, you could still hear her screaming, "Please, please, don't leave me in here."

I'd become "them" – the enemy – and I knew if I stayed at the Center one day longer, I would lose the little consciousness I'd collected with much effort, and perhaps, my soul as well.

I walked back to the little prison, opened the door, and saw the twelve-year-old girl lying in a fetal position. I opened the door slowly, sat down in the doorway, keeping the door propped open with my body.

"I won't leave you in here alone."

"You promise?" she said wiping the tears away.

"I promise, and I'll never put you in here ever again."

"Thank you, thank you, you fucker," she said half-smiling, half-testing, and half-teasing, hoping it was the truth, but almost sure, it was just a trick.

I sat down with her for about ten or fifteen minutes and then escorted her back to the group, and gave each of them a hug, and walked into the supervising psychiatrist's office and said, "I quit."

"I understand. Why don't you consider going to med school? I can get you into any one you choose with the recommendation I'll write for you, then specialize in psychiatry, and then you'll have a more powerful voice to tell people like me and the staff your way of doing things, even though to be clear, I don't agree with most of them. I do however recognize passion for helping people when I see it" he said.

I told him thanks for the offer and the backhanded compliment but that I knew if I did what he suggested and since I'd felt like an outsider all of my life among family, friends, and colleagues that I'd become accustomed to going my own way.

Since then, I've keynoted over one hundred clinical conferences, consulted at treatment centers, established a training program for counselors that lasted twenty-eight years, and opened and was director of the Austin Men's Center.

Well let's just say over the last nearly four decades I've looked at, thought about, and written numerous books on how to think differently about many of the things we have been taught or been told about human behavior, relationships, men's issues, recovery, and other matters.

Having presented the matters that you're about to read (I hope) to therapists, social workers, counselors, and the general public, and getting pretty good responses, I decided to put this compilation of outsider ideas, tools, and information in this little book. I hope it helps.

PART I

THINKING ABOUT THINGS DIFFERENTLY

Are We Afraid or Anxious?

*"If I take death into my life, acknowledge it,
and face it squarely, I will free myself from the anxiety of
death and the pettiness of life—
and only then will I be free to become myself."*
Martin Heidegger

I have been talking for some time now about the differences between depression and despair. For me to really work with my own despair or really listen to anyone's, I have to be connected to the anxiety that I have numbed with alcohol, work addiction, love addiction, and thus avoided, suppressed and discounted, and most of all, confused with fear all the while being diagnosed and treated for depression. Freud tells us that anxiety "is a riddle whose solution would be bound to throw a floodlight on our whole mental existence."

Anxiety, unlike fear, has no external source, cause, or cure, unlike it's near relative, fear. Fear has an object. If I'm afraid of flying, which I used to be, talk therapy and immersion therapy and then getting in a plane can make the fear disappear. If I'm afraid of the dark, then I just keep the lights on. If I'm afraid of lions, then I don't go to the jungle or the park; but the anxiety that comes from being on the planet and confronting my mortality is amorphous, ephemeral, but just as damn real as any lion. Kierkegaard says, "Whereas fear sharpens the senses, unrecognized anxiety dulls the spirit" as well as the soul and creativity, not to mention any connection to something divine if that is what one is searching for. Once fear is identified I can fly, fight, or freeze. Anxiety is a disorder of desire for something that we can't put a name to and can't see, taste, hear or smell but everyone knows it is there if we just get quiet enough. The dictionary says, "Fear is an unpleasant emotion caused by the belief that someone or something is dangerous, likely to cause pain or a threat." The dictionary goes on to say anxiety "is a feeling of worry, nervousness, a dis-ease about an uncertain outcome."

The philosopher Karl Jaspers speaks of anxiety this way, "a feeling of restlessness… a feeling that one… has not finished something… or that one has to look for something." After my divorce I went to my quiet, windy mountain cottage to look at my anxiety right in the eye because I have been anxious my whole life. The Catholic monk and mystic Thomas Merton wants us to know, "anxiety is the mark of spiritual insecurity."

One of the deepest forms of anxiety is "disintegration

anxiety." This is the anxiety that something or someone might destroy our inner-most self, and to put it simply, we don't know what is going to happen to us in the future except death for certain and then what?

When the preacher that baptized me over on Sand Mountain when I was nine years old and laid his bony hand on my shoulder and pronounced that I'd be a preacher, I started asking myself, my mom, my god, preachers and priests what to do and not do. However, Merton goes on to say anxiety comes from "being afraid to ask the right questions because they might turn out to have no answer."

So, am I finally, at the tender age of 68, poised to start asking the right questions? Am I ready to follow the Christian theologian Paul Tillich's advice who says one of the cures for my despair and anxiety is to "believe you are accepted" and to accept myself questions, despair, bone loneliness and all?

The post-modern novelist, Walk Percy, says "Anxiety summons us to an authentic experience," and if I strip down to all that I have learned, felt, seen, and heard, then one way to move out of despair and anxiety is to strip away as many false selves that have been created over the decades in my on-going search for happiness.

Are you afraid or anxious? Even though these words are used interchangeably by very intelligent people, I hope after reading this it may help you sort it out as I continue to do so.

"Anxiety is altogether different from fear and similar concepts..."

Soren Kierkegaard

Eros and Thanatos: Passion and Death

"Friend, hope for the Guest while you are alive..."
Kabir, translated by Robert Bly

Most of my adult life, both professionally and personally, has been devoted to a pursuit of Eros, which means "life instinct," passion, purpose, and positivity. Eros is the drive to live fully.

My bouts with alcoholism over the decades were a movement towards death and away from Eros. Addiction is an unconscious relationship with Thanatos – the drive toward death and destruction. When I was younger, I used to drive my cars like death did not matter, but in reality, it was Thanatos in the passenger seat next to me whispering, "go faster."

Why am I writing about these two concepts – Eros and Thanatos? Because our country is drowning in the river Styx for many reasons, including a sore lack of life-preserving and life-affirming leadership.

Many men and women not wearing masks or social

distancing think they are acting out of the life instinct and a desire for freedom. "Freedom's just another word for nothing left to lose," and according to Bob Dylan freedom to die and kill others is not true freedom because it is in bondage to Thanatos.

The people who refuse to do what they can to stop the spread of Virus/Thanatos to others (especially the older generation which includes me and many of you reading this right now) don't even know or perhaps do not care they are participating in the drive towards death – not life.

How many more people, young and old, have to die before we as a society and individuals agree to worship the drive to Life and stop our reckless disregard for the lives of others? When will we become adults who feel passionate again and in love with Eros, in love with life?

Perhaps we should all agree to take the physician's vow – "First do no harm" – while Thanatos is taking lives.

"I celebrate myself, and sing myself,
And what I assume you shall assume…"

Walt Whitman Philosophy

"Caring for" Someone or "Care taking" Someone Makes a Big Difference

"...teach us to care, and not to care and to be still..."

T.S. Eliot

Last week I was honored to be invited to speak to about a hundred folks at a Co-dependents Anonymous meeting in California. I told them, among other things, that one way I continue to work with my own and my clients' tendencies to put other people's needs and feelings before theirs or mine to my detriment and exhaustion is to keep making the distinction between "caring for" someone and "care taking" someone.

While I explain the differences more fully in my new book, **The Flying Boy Letters: Getting Back to Y'all 30 Years Later**, I want to give a shorter version here — "Care taking" is usually done out of a sense of guilt, obligation, or duty. We feel like we don't have a choice and anytime there is the feeling of choice-less-ness, there is likely going to be some regression involved where we are hurled back to childhood when we didn't have a lot of choices.

"Caring for" is most often going to leave us feeling grateful that we can be of help and support while "care taking" is tiring, exhausting and more often than not creates some resentment and even anger because we would rather be doing something else with our limited time and energy. "Caring for" leaves us energized, fulfilled, and even joyful. We feel like compassionate adults who consciously make a decision to comfort, nurture, help or be there for someone in some kind of way.

Most of us were raised with the terrible notion that because someone is biologically related to us that we must or are supposed to "take care" of them even if it is draining us and keeping us from living our lives. Also, interestingly, the one receiving the "care taking" can feel "one down," infantilized, patronized, and less than the one providing "care taking" and often are guilty of feeling little or no gratitude.

"Caring for" comes out of compassion and love, and "care taking" comes out of guilt – trying to be a "people pleaser."

Novelist Eleanor Brown wrote, "Self-care is not selfish. You cannot serve from an empty vessel."

Designated Problem: Let's Get Rid of the Label

"Everything that irritates us about others can lead us to an understanding about ourselves."

C.G. Jung

"Mend his life." "You really need help." "Fix her." "If he would just get into therapy." "If she would only stop drinking." "We'd be all right then."

No, you wouldn't be, and neither would they. You see, one of the greatest barriers for people to overcome is being the "Designated Problem" in the family, marriage, or workplace.

The label impedes the growth and healing of everyone concerned. When all the focus and attention is put on the alcoholic, addict, non-communicator, the one unable to be in touch with their feelings or their reality – that's just too much weight on anybody's shoulders. The shame, embarrassment, and guilt are enough to make anyone unable to really change.

For over 35 years I've worked with angry, depressed, aggressive, traumatized men and women, and one of the first things I do is help them see the truth: that it is the system, dynamic or context that is the real culprit.

You see, even if the Problem Person does deep psychological, emotional, and spiritual work and grows and changes, if he or she goes back to a toxic workplace, an untreated family, or a dysfunctional marriage, he or she will soon be the Designated Problem again, and again break everyone's heart and hope.

For decades I was the designated problem in my family— the outcast, black sheep, troublemaker, alcoholic. No wonder my shoulders were bowed to the ground all through my 20s.

Lord, the therapy and recovery I had to do to lift that burden!

I wrote about my work in the men's and recovery movements in **The Flying Boy: Healing the Wounded Man and Flying Boy Book II: The Journey Continues** and aired my family's less than clean laundry and my own problems with relationships, alcohol, and not knowing a feeling if it bit me on the ass. My dad and I didn't speak for ten years; he was so angry. Back then I was beginning to see that there was more to these problems than just me, my dad, or my girlfriends.

"We" are the problem – wife as well as husband, children, grandparents, and even the babysitter. We all are the problem.

Most of us, I know I did, have to turn to an objective, third-party like a therapist, coach, sponsor, who can help to more readily identify each person's patterns of behaviors, problems, histories, hang-ups and character defects, and I promise the formerly so-called Designated Problem will get better – indeed we all will.

So, when you think you are, or they are the sick ones remember Rumi's words: "The fault is in the blamer. Spirit sees nothing to criticize."

Closure: A Made-Up Relationship Term

If you're going home for the holidays, trying to recover from a divorce, a breakup or really any transition, change or loss may I suggest we stop looking for Closure.

Closure is, according to the dictionary, "a psychological term that describes an individual's desire for a firm answer to a question and an aversion to ambiguity." And it is a "set has closure under an operation if performance of that operation on members of the set…" I never understood math or calculus and people are not mathematical equations. And just because we long for lost love, happier childhoods, better outcomes of all kinds and what we wish would be never gets finished like a math problem or a business deal. The idea of closure is a therapist's shell game – find the closure pea under one of three cups. The therapeutic community tries hard to not know there was never any pea in the first place. Closure is a made up modern psychological word. It probably came into use sometime in the 60s. Perhaps Gestalt therapy, Primal, EST, later Forum, and Insight, all agreed we should seek this state in order to move on. Moving on does not require closure.

You see after each failed relationship, no matter how bitter or sweet the ending, we still think about them when we see someone who looks like them in an airport. On a holiday we see them in the window of a passing Toyota, and if we don't see them there, we see them in our dreams or at the very least, when we hear "our song" on the radio.

My first love, mostly unrequited, on-again-off-again, high school and college sweetheart and lifetime friend got married very young to a very unkind man. However, we saw each other at class reunions, funerals, weddings and sometimes late at night when neither of us could sleep we'd call and talk for hours. No matter how many hours of therapy I did looking for this enigmatic, amorphous thing called closure, I never found it. However, we explored the option of being together for decades. The closest thing to it was the four hours we spent in a Hampton Inn in downtown Austin when she learned she would be leaving this world thanks to the curse of cancer. We sat down and told each other everything in-between loud sobs, laughter and watching the other customers nervously leave the restaurant. You know I still think about her. I'm writing a novel with her as the main character. Now anyone reading this might think I need more therapy and you'd be right – one can never get enough says this therapist of 35 years and counting.

For those of you who like hard research – 3,000 men and women were asked on a questionnaire would they consider remarrying their ex-spouse if they were available? Seventy percent said they would definitely consider it. So much for closure. Do you know how many people marry their high-school or college sweetheart after their spouse dies? Me either, but it is quite a few.

Okay literature and movie aficionados look at literary books published before the 60s. Steinbeck's Joad family did not find closure in California, no closure in Hemingway, Fitzgerald and certainly none in Faulkner, Hawthorne or Mark Twain, and there is not even any in the Bible.

"Oh, Rhett, why can't we just get closure?" "Frankly, my dear I don't give a damn…"

Bogart and Bacall or Spencer Tracy never found it.

Hans Solo never even thought to ask.

Even Butch and Sundance remain frozen in time.

Finally, I bet you never heard your grandparents or parents, if you are over 40, use the "C" word.

The bottom line, some people leave us, and some people come back, and some leave us again and the parents, siblings, former best friends aren't now who they were; they are ghosts that still haunt us, memories of who and what they were like and how things used to be like or never were. If one of my best friends, who left me for reasons unknown was to appear today at my door she could never close up the sorrow of the she who left. If my father, who is still alive at 93, and I tried to get "closure" with the 30-year-old father he was, it would be impossible. That young, green father is dead and gone. The feelings we have that make us seek closure are coming from memories we have of the past and the illusions we have of our futures should go.

SOLUTIONS

1. A line from a Robert Bly poem, "The people we have loved, we will always love…"

2. Use your therapy money to help you find resolution – oh wait, that is Closure's kissing cousin, never mind.

3. The word closure originated from the word "enclosure" and that is what we really do at the end of a relationship. We build an enclosure in our hearts and at the same time we let go as best as we can, and never let anyone tell you when you have grieved too long.

Why We Can't Be Rejected

"When we lose someone and we find ourselves, we win."

Anonymous

One of my best, dearest friends I'll call K has broken all contact. She doesn't call; she doesn't write; she doesn't send flowers or return texts, and seemingly doesn't miss me at all. My psychologist brain says, "don't take it personally." My human heart says, "she has rejected me, and it hurts." But here's the truth. You and I can be dismissed, avoided, shunned, hell even banished but we cannot be rejected.

You readers will say, "Well you're just wrong. My boyfriend rejected me last week." "My father has always rejected me." "My best friend hasn't spoken to me in over a year. Don't tell me she hasn't rejected me."

No one can reject us. Here's why – because it's never about us. We are the creators of not only our outer worlds but our interior ones as well and what we are drawn to or deny is already in us lying loose, latent or floating down that ole' river D-nial.

I was well into my 50s, having "felt" and "thought" I'd been rejected numerous times before it became clear to me, thanks in large part due to my long-time therapist and mentor, Dr. James Maynard.

You see, I lived my relationship life foolishly thinking that if I was attracted to a girlfriend or other loved ones it was because something was in them that was not in me – that perhaps it was their lovely disposition that pulled me into their orbit. They were "attractive" because of their looks, spirituality, intelligence, groundedness, sense of humor, etc. all things that my low self-esteem told me I lacked.

What James and decades of experiences showed me was that real attraction for others, and they to me, emanates from within and goes out to them. Attraction thus is self-generated, rather than coming from the other person and when I'm no longer attracted to someone or I've integrated their qualities, I stop generating the interest in them, but I do not reject them nor they me.

This truth becomes obvious I hope in Rumi's poem:

"... Lovers don't
Finally meet somewhere, they've been
in each other all along."
Translated by Coleman Barks

Those we love who we think are rejecting us are rejecting those things in themselves they are no longer able to pull out of their own inner or outer shadowy part of themselves that they projected onto us.

A woman I loved a long time ago and am still good friends with I'll call B, was extremely intelligent and cleaned houses for a living when I met her while giving a lecture at a local university. She was also a nurturer, mother and possessed boundless sexual energy. I was a counselor, writer, still too much in my head and anything but a nurturing, parenting person, with little to no domestic inclinations at the time. Of course, we got together. During those four years later, I became a pretty good stepfather with a greater inclination to nurture, and after we went to many therapy sessions we broke up. Once again at first, I thought she had rejected me. To make a long story short she went back to school and got a master's degree in counseling psychology and is one of the best working therapists.

A couple of years later I got married to Susan, bought a home and we set out to have children that hopefully I would spend a lot more time with than I would in hotels and conference centers.

Going back to K – she left, either because she saw things in me that she was not ready to embrace in herself or already had successfully embraced or perhaps never needed and therefore I guess I rejected the "sunny" disposition she had in abundance while I was grieving my despairing divorce. She rejected my "old age" and perhaps I rejected the youth she possessed but was still somewhere in me even though I was having a terrible time finding it. She rejected my seriousness, and damn-it, I rejected the spontaneity I saw in her that I have always longed to have more of and on and on. Our paths diverged because I needed to access all that she manifested, and she either needed to access some of what she saw in me, but to be clear, neither of us did anything wrong nor did we "reject" the other.

In my book, **Writing From the Body**, I said that people tend to be drawn to artists because they dream of being creative, but they've been told that they are not, or they are afraid to succeed or fail having way too many credit cards, cars and a house payment they feel they must pay off first. However, "If we spot it, we got it," as the old AA saying goes. So, we tend to "acquire" the artistic creative person instead of "accessing" the artist, writer, or the tender, compassionate domestic, nurturing, sexy person we've been all along.

So, the next time you or I "feel" rejected see the Solutions below:

1. Make a list of the qualities, characteristics, attitudes, traits you have found in others and acknowledge and further develop them in yourself.
2. Remember the attraction for others starts inside you and proceeds outwards, and as the Indian poet Kabir says, "I say to my inner lover, why such a rush..." because I say he or she has always been inside us waiting for us to stop projecting onto others.

The Illusion and Reality of Abandonment

Years ago I said to the dismay of more than 500 of the attendees at a clinical conference in Florida: "Adults can't be abandoned." They were stunned and contemplating tarring and feathering me and running me out of town.

"Wait a minute – I didn't say adults can't feel abandoned." A mother says, "But my adult son stopped coming to see me. He abandoned me." "My wife abandoned me 30 years ago," a client said to me in a therapy session. Actually, I've heard, "They abandoned me," hundreds of times.

But you see adults don't get left on the steps of an orphanage or at the door of a police station, and they don't end up in a mall holding the hands of the security guard looking for mommy or daddy.

Most children after the Industrial Revolution, and even now, experience a variety of forms of temporary or permanent abandonment. Fifty percent of households in the U.S. is a one-parent home, and a one- or even two-person home will in fact leave their children unattended for brief to long periods – not maliciously – but cooking, cleaning, phone ringing, doorbells ringing and 30- to 40-hour work weeks.

In order to not experience abandonment, there needs to be an extended family, caregivers, etc. to meet a child's needs every hour of every day. Remember 20 minutes in a soiled diaper or crying hungry in a crib feels like eternity.

When someone leaves us, a husband, wife, lover, or even a good friend, we may enter into "Child Time." A non-returned phone call on Monday leaves us feeling like 24 hours is 24 days by Tuesday.

Many reading this have been abandoned so many times

in childhood and adolescence that we become habituated to constantly abandoning our essential self. We give ourselves away to be with someone for fear if we don't, then someone will leave us and never come back.

Bottom line – we as adults abandon ourselves quite frequently until we don't, and once we learn how to keep ourselves when another adult leaves us, we will feel loss, grief, anger, disappointment, despair and depression but we won't feel "abandoned" because we are connected to our deepest self.

Here are some ways to stay connected:

1. Learn more and more ways to implement self-care and self-soothing.
2. Bring in any or many supportive friends to be with you as you come out of "Child Time."
3. See a counselor, therapist, priest, rabbi, etc.
4. Get out in nature as much as possible.
5. Cry, scream into your pillow, write "loss letters."

I hope this helps.

Are You Empathetic or Sympathetic?
There's a Big Difference

"...Tell me about your despair,
And I'll tell you about mine..."

Mary Oliver

While nothing much is as black and white as things sound, for the purposes of discussion, here are the definitions.

Empathy: I understand some of what you are feeling and going through because I've been through similar experiences myself.

Sympathy: I feel what you feel. If you're sad, I'm sad. If you're angry, I'm angry. If you're happy so am I.

As a trainer of therapists and the general public for over 35 years I've been teaching the differences. You see with all due respect; I don't want or need to feel what you feel. You don't need my sympathy unless a loved one has died. But I damn sure want to do my best to empathize with your pain or problems and what you are going through.

In my very early years as a counselor, I thought I was supposed to feel your pain in my own body. That is what I'd been doing since early childhood – feeling my mother's pain. Therapists who don't know the difference will experience burn out pretty quickly. You see we all have enough pain or problems and thus we don't want yours to seep into our bodies and souls.

Now if you have young children or aging or infirmed loved ones who cannot articulate their needs, then sympathy is absolutely necessary. However, if your kids are 12 or over, ideally you will switch to empathy with them because if you are still "feeling" their pain and hurts and disappointments they will struggle to separate themselves from you in healthy or less than healthy ways.

You see if we tend to feel what other adults feel that can tend to regress them, shrink them, and make them feel small, and perhaps unable to feel their own feelings for fear they are causing us to feel uncomfortable.

Bottom line – Empathy elevates, lifts others up, and sometimes temporarily or permanently lifts them out of their feelings and confirms that they can deal with whatever is going on inside them or outside of them.

So, sympathy tends to shrink, and empathy tends to elevate. Many men and women identify and think of themselves as "empaths," but based on the above definition when you or I feel what another adult feels, we are "sympaths."

Many highly intellectually intelligent people confuse the two terms and some even use them interchangeably as if they mean the same thing, but they don't. Emotionally intelligent people empathize.

"Oh, the comfort—
The inexpressible comfort of feeling
safe with a person..."

George Eliot

Feeling Guilty: Maybe Not

"Guilt is a teacher, love is the lesson."

Joan Borysenko, Ph.D.

Guilt is not a feeling. Guilt is a judgement and a social/ religious construct that has been drilled into our heads for so long that we actually think we "feel guilty" a good deal of the time.

I ask my clients and workshop participants to tell me where they feel their guilt in their bodies. Their faces turn into question marks; but when I ask where they hold anger, sadness, fear, joy, and love, they point to their stomachs, shoulders, backs, jaws, or hearts.

Guilt then is a way to shut down or numb our feelings.

Cindy says, "I don't want to invite my alcoholic sister to

have Christmas with us this year. But I'll 'feel guilty' if I don't. She'll be all alone and will probably just stay drunk."

"But what do you really feel about her drinking and coming to your home that way? Are you angry, sad, or scared for your sister?" I asked her in a session.

"Yes, all of the above," she said.

When I was growing up if my parents heard something like Cindy didn't ask her sister to Christmas they would have thought/said she was being selfish and should feel guilty. Which, looking back was code that if I didn't come home from Christmas someday I "should feel guilty" and years ago I would have. Self-Care were not words used in our family back then in the dark ages.

Now, don't get me wrong. If I steal from you or slander your good name or abuse you in some way and the poisonous snake in our heads, we'll call the Guilt Snakes hiss at us and bite into our brains then we must chop their heads off by admitting we were wrong, make apologies and amends, and make restitution out of our regret and remorse. This removes the snakes by putting them back in the garden where they belong. Remember, speaking of the Garden, and Adam and Eve (Adam in Greek means "man" and Eve means "woman") – neither of them felt guilty about their nakedness but rather felt joyful at the freedom and ecstasy until someone told them they should feel guilty and grab some fig leaves. That's a lot of guilt leaves in almost every household.

So, guilt, while not a feeling, says we've done something wrong and we need to put on clothes of compassion to make things right, we must not let it override our true feelings and learn how to express them appropriately. Now shame says we are "wrong, broken, damaged, beyond repair," but that's a whole other blog.

> *"You do not have to be good.*
> *You do not have to walk on your knees*
> *for a hundred miles through*
> *the desert repenting..."*

Mary Oliver

They Love You – In Their Own Way

When I was a boy, the conversation went something like this: "Mom, does dad love me?"

"Of course, he does son, in his own way."

"Then why doesn't he show it or tell me he loves me?

"He just can't son but trust me he does."

As a young adult the conversation would often go like this: "John, do you love me?"

"Sure, I do. You know I do."

"Then why don't you ever tell me you love me?"

"Why do you keep asking me? I'm here ain't I?"

A whole lot of people young and old don't get loved the way they need. Many good people try to practice the "Golden Rule" when it comes to love: "Do unto others the way you would have them do unto you." Not bad! But what happens if they treat you the way they want to be treated, loved, adored, cherished, and respected?

So, for some time (though I have failed many times) I try to practice what I call "The Platinum Rule:" Do unto others the way they have been longing probably their whole lives.

In other words, send your loved ones and show your loved ones the love they need instead of the way we wanted to be loved by our mothers, fathers, lovers, ex-girlfriends, or past husbands, wives, and yes, even our children.

When I ask my clients, who are wrestling with love, "How do you want to be loved?" More often than not (especially men) will say, "I don't know. No one has ever asked me that question and I've never asked myself."

Then I might say, "Have you ever asked your loved ones how they want to be loved?"

"No, but they all know I love them in my own way."

One client said, "Well I don't want to tell them how I want to be loved. They should know after all this time. If you have to ask, then it doesn't count."

One time I said in response, "If I ask you to buy a new Volvo and you say yes and you do, do you think I'm going to say take it back because I had to ask you?" Hell, no! I'll drive it with a smile.

"Alright then," as we say in the South:

1. Become aware of how you want to be loved.
2. Ask your loved ones how they want to be loved.
3. Tell everyone you really love what makes you feel loved.
4. Occasionally ask your loved ones this question, "How well am loving you?"
   And then, to quote the great American wise man, James Taylor, "Shower the people you love with love…"

Are You Feeling Melancholy?

"Besides my numerous circle of acquaintances, I have one more intimate confidant – my melancholy... My melancholy is the most faithful mistress I have known..."

Soren Kierkegaard

The word "melancholy" is no longer used much these days, sad to say. So exactly what does the word mean? There is no exact answer, but here are my ruminations and reflections on this under-used, misunderstood word.

Melancholy is a particular species of sadness. It isn't an illness or a mental problem – it's just part of the human condition. Melancholy tends to involve the pleasure of reflection and contemplation of the things we love, lost or long for. The author, Susan Sontag, says: "Depression is melancholy minus its charms."

The word that best describes melancholy is the word "missingness," if that indeed is a word. Missingness is a longing for an absent something. It is a momentary emptiness and a combination of sadness and perhaps even some happiness. Missingness or melancholy is a wistful longing and yearning for the return of something gone.

On the day I wrote this, I was listening to the Righteous Brothers,' "Unchained Melody." I longed to be in my old friend's living room when we were thirteen. Bob would sing

along with these "Blue-Eyed Soul" brothers and I swear
he could switch from tenor to low base with elegant ease
just like the duo could. It was a sight and sound to be held
close to my heart but without depression, just melancholy
missingness. Bob has been gone now for a long time.

While melancholy is no substitute for feelings of sorrow,
sadness, grief, or loss, it does carry some amount of energy
and creativity for me whereas depression is exhausting.
It has always been the midnight oil I burn so I can write.
Melancholy is a kind of white magic that allows artists
to paint, sculpt, play music – listen sometimes to Samuel
Barber's "Adagio for Strings" and let the melancholy wash
over you.

Lastly, too much solitude can cause melancholy ("Saturday
night and I ain't got nobody…" Sam Cooke) and sometimes
my melancholy aches for solitude and if I don't find it, it can
turn into loneliness.

Melancholy is my speed of light time machine into the past
and my path into my more creative self where I can yearn,
become wistful and comforted.

> *"I can barely conceive of a type of beauty*
> *in which there is no melancholy."*
>
> Charles Baudelaire

Regression: The Damage

"Where have all the grownups gone?"
Robert Bly, *The Sibling Society*

Emotional regression is a personal and social unconscious return to our history when our buttons are pushed, or we get triggered, and we react instead of responding. Regression gives us the sense that we are small or little and not the powerful adults we are much of the time.

When we regress, we leave our new brain, our prefrontal lobe and hide in the limbic brain until the threat and emotional or physical harm has passed. It is in this very old part of our brain that we only have three choices – fight, flight, or freeze. Any one or all of these choices are usually adolescent, infantile, and primal.

When I wrote my book, **Growing Yourself Back Up: Understanding Emotional Regression**, I focused solely on how regression in our personal lives usually equaled regret. Regressed men and women will say or not say, do or not do or let be done that we may regret for days, weeks, or even decades. Trust me; I know; I've seen my own regressions too many times. That's why I wrote the book as well as to help others with this misunderstood state of mind. I'm sad to recall one time something my then-wife said, and I took my wedding ring off and threw it across the room. I remember it as if it were yesterday and I still regret it.

With all of this said, I want to turn my attention to the undeniable regression that our society is in – a mass regressed, unconscious, adolescent, and infantile state as I've ever witnessed. We are in a collective trance spun by malignant hypnotists.

Alright! Enough! We must leave their trance knowing we've lost touch with our feelings, our bodies and souls. We must leave our limbic brain and head back to the halls of our hearts and Congress by way of non-violence and stop acting, shooting, hood-wearing, and hate spewing.

How do we do it? Here's what I said for coming out of regression in our personal relations and perhaps these will apply to our social interactions:

1. Get attention from our support system.

2. Get and give empathy and compassion from those who understand.

3. Release the hurt, tears, fears, angers, sadness's we've stored in our bodies and collective psyches.

4. Pray, meditate, march to stop the terrorists in their tracks.

   "What do you think of Western Civilization?"
   "I think it would be a good idea," said Gandhi.

Honesty: Brutal, Rigorous Lying

*"Are you proud of yourself tonight that you have insulted a
total stranger whose circumstances you know nothing about?"*

Atticus Finch – To Kill a Mockingbird

On the 4th of July, a new acquaintance and I had lunch
and it went very well. However, in the parking lot as we were
saying goodbye she said, "I need to tell you the truth about
something.

"Go ahead," I said.

She replied, "It's going to be brutal."

Now for some set of reasons, I said, "go ahead." Let's just
say I was caught off guard and quite taken with her. We might
say here in the South that I was smitten.

Here's what I wish I had said, and would normally say to
someone, anyone who starts to tell a truth beginning with the
adjective, "brutal." "No thank you, not today," or "Stop, I'll
be glad to hear a rigorous truth, but I try not to be brutal –
I've had enough brutality for this lifetime."

So, what's the difference? Brutal is going to be about me,
not you. Brutal is always going to contain some level of
shaming, criticizing, belittling, or demeaning words. Hers
contained all of these.

42

On the other hand, a rigorous truth is going to tell you about them – what they need, want, or don't want.

In the case of my acquaintance, she wanted me to stop calling her "hon," or "dear," or "darling."

Rigorous would have been something like, "I'm uncomfortable," or "those words don't work for me," or "I feel patronized," any would have been honest, sincere, and vulnerable and require my deepest respect.

Brutal honesty, by the way, is kissing cousins with the prefaces, "with all due respect," or "I mean no disrespect," or "I hope you won't take offense," or "I'm telling you this, but I hope you won't take it personally." All these are requiring the responses like, "No, thank you," or "I'm not going to be shamed today."

Now a word about honesty and lying. If someone pulls out a photo of their grandchild, baby, or wiener dog, or hairless cat and they say, "Isn't she beautiful" or "the cutest thing you've ever seen?" Well, any good Southerner should lie their face off and say, "Why, yes, hon, that little dear is the prettiest, most beautiful thing I've ever seen, darlin,'" and make sure you look as honest and sincere as Atticus Finch, the lawyer in "To Kill a Mockingbird."

*"People who are brutally honest
get more satisfaction out of the brutality
than out of the honesty."*

Richard J. Weedham

Boundaries
We Have to Watch Out Where We're Going:
Boundary Errors and Boundary Violations

First, a boundary is "This is how close you can come to me" physically, spiritually, in conversations about love or money, etc.

A "boundary error" is when someone, whether friend or foe, has crossed over into my space, my yard, my soul, or my pasture because they didn't notice the "No Trespassing" sign or signal. As the poet William Stafford says, "The signals we give should be clear. The darkness around us is deep." Or, as Robert Frost less dramatically put it, "Good fences make good neighbors." A boundary error is simply a mistake made more or less innocently. When informed, the perpetrators can see or hear their errors and can apologize and vow to be respectful in the future.

On the other hand, is the "boundary violation." This is committed when a person has been informed and warned, often numerous times, what your particular boundaries are in a certain situation, but keeps pushing and pressing in on the boundaries you have communicated. This is when the person will not respect those boundaries and, to some lesser or greater degree, knows that it irritates you, frustrates you, or makes you angry. This person might justify and rationalize their unwanted behavior and say that they are just "teasing," "playing," or "kidding" while telling you to "lighten up." In truth, the above behaviors are just passive-aggressive pebbles in your shoe as you walk through the relationship. Or worse violations feel like boulders on your head or stabs to the heart.

What to do and what to say depends on who it is and in what context you feel those errors or violations are committed. Generally, boundary errors get committed once and are willingly corrected. Boundary violators get two warnings, and on the third time you may have to start rethinking your relationship to the violator, whether a boss, friend, family, lover, or spouse.

The really sad thing is that many people don't know what boundaries are, don't have very good boundaries themselves, and often confuse boundaries with walls. Where good boundaries exist, walls are not necessary. Boundaries—done appropriately—increase intimacy and communication and reduce conflict and confrontations.

Here are a few common examples. People think that it is okay to talk about other peoples' bodies. I have a beautiful friend who gets told by complete strangers, "You're too thin!" or, "Are you eating enough?" Pregnant women get their bellies touched by complete strangers. Babies get pinched on the cheek. One friend had to stop a woman he'd never even seen before from putting a sock back on his very young son.

The real remedy? Ask before touching. Get information. Don't assume—you know what that does. Tell folks your boundaries and tell them when they've committed errors, so they won't turn into violations, and get really acquainted with your own boundaries.

The Differences Between Depression and Despair

"Despair is a haven with its own temporary form of beauty..."
David Whyte

Several years ago, I gave a brief lecture to about a hundred men at a conference in Minnesota on the differences between depression and despair. During the talk, a tall man standing in the back of the room began weeping. At the end of my forty-five-minute presentation I asked the man if he was okay, and would he mind sharing what brought him to tears?

"For twenty-five years I have been telling my wife she had to do something, get some help or something for her depression. We fought over this a hundred times and every time she would say something like, 'You just don't understand. It's not depression. It's something else,' and I would let it go for a while and then we'd get into it again. I have to go home and apologize to her and try to make amends because now after your talk I know what she was trying to tell me but just didn't have the words. Now I know it is, and always has been, despair."

A few years later after my divorce I went to my cabin in the Appalachian Mountains to deal with my own adult despair, not my childhood, adolescence, or young adult depression. It was in that house that I read everything I could on despair. When I wasn't reading or weeping, I stared for hours out windows and into some distant pastures, past ponds and pine trees and slowly the distinction between depression and despair came into view. Even though many educated and thoughtful people and professionals use these two words interchangeably I came to fully realize they were as different as night and day.

Depression is a biological and emotional quest for light, relief, and balance. Depression gives nothing and takes everything—sleep, food, relationships, and much more.

Despair on the other hand seeks darkness, like that of St. John of the Cross in his beautiful work, "Dark Night of the Soul," or in the case of the Babylonian myth of the great flood. In this version of Noah and the flood the hero of the story wants desperately to know if there is any dry land to be found so he sends out birds—a sparrow, dove and they don't return with any news at all, but the last bird he sends out is the crow and it returns with mud on its feet. When we're in despair we are searching for the mud in our minds, art, hearts, careers, parenting, and partnering hoping to find meaning, usefulness and authenticity.

Depression does nothing to remove the masks we've made and worn for a lifetime. Despair's desire is to take the ego, the personas and all the false selves and drown them under 40 days and 40 nights, or in my case, over 40 years and watch them sink to the bottom of the flooded false self. Despair is desperate to find the truth of our existence here on earth.

Here is a little more light about the differences between depression and despair. First, depression is a situational, circumstantial, or biochemical imbalance or a combination of all three. Change the situation, the circumstances for the better and the depression should diminish, dissipate, or disappear. If it is due to biochemical difficulties, then change the biochemistry and the depression should lessen. What we know is that only two out of ten people who are diagnosed with depression get little or no relief from pharmacology or psychotherapy or both. What is the other eight or millions really suffering from? Could it be despair that pills, nor PhDs or psychiatrists cannot cure?

Despair is rooted in an existential loneliness that almost everyone is afraid to admit for fear they have done something wrong. Despair is a house we eventually have to sit in until we are ready to reassess our deepest self and our interior world. It is in this house where we must unabashedly and without embarrassment or shame strip away all our false selves. Despair is the first stage of freedom and an entrance into a more genuine and real existence. Despair is the bridge that takes us from "here to there." Despair is that lonesome valley that we all fear but must be walked through. It is the dissonance or the distance between what we thought we would do with this life and what we have actually done, who we thought we'd be and who we became.

Despair is caused by self-betrayal and giving up on our deepest desires; it is the result of the risks not taken, the love not received or spoken. As John Burnside said, "Nothing I know matters more than what never happened." Despair is the continual frustration and even anger over the feeling that some unspoken or spoken contract or agreement with our self, each other or the divine has been broken or dishonored. It is very different from depression and must be treated differently.

In the words of poet Mary Oliver, "...tell me about your despair, and I'll tell you about mine." Or as David Whyte says, "...I want to know if you belong or feel abandoned, if you can know despair or see it in others."

So, I ask you to think a little differently now and consider, is it depression or despair that you wrestle with?

"Life begins on the other side of despair."

Jean Paul Sartre

Identifying Passivity

Passivity is a compulsion or learned tendency to live at half-speed regarding certain segments of our lives. Almost no one reading this is "purely" passive but rather exhibiting passive tendencies which ultimately leaves people feeling their life or career glass is half-empty and thus halfheartedly committing to projects, plans, and goals. Passive people are half in and half out of relationships. The passive person who suffers the effects of a *half-lived life* is more attached to not having what they think they want or desire, even though they protest loudly this is not so.

A client of mine, James, is 40 and a very successful real estate agent who earns a high six-figure income. During a session he said, "I work all the time on my marriage. I'm in therapy; I read books and I regularly attend self-help work-shops. No one can say I'm passive." When asked about his marriage he quickly replied, "I want more physical contact, more touching, and yes, more sex, but I hardly get any at all."

James wants his wife, Brenda, to be more affectionate and yet he indulges in a whole host of behaviors that guarantees he won't get this and actually gets him just the opposite of what he thinks and says he wants.

I asked him to give me an example of his efforts to get affection from his wife so I could see and show him his passivity and addiction to not having what he says he wants.

James said, "I go into the living room all the time and Brenda is on the couch watching television for hours on end. I say something like, 'Can't you turn that thing off for a little while? There's nothing intelligent or worth watching on TV. I don't know why you watch these silly shows.' But she never agrees, and I end up storming out of the room frustrated as usual."

I jokingly said, "How's that working for you?" Then I offered a suggestion. "Try sitting on the living room couch next to her; gently lifting her legs and placing them on your lap while you massage her feet, instead of shaming, criticizing, demeaning, and judging her. Then simply ask her what's on that you two can watch together."

He looked at me like I was speaking in a foreign tongue; in a way it was an unfamiliar language because it was the language of compassionate assertiveness.

James looked a little dumbfounded. "No, I have never even thought of it. It sounds so simple. Why didn't this ever occur to me before?" he said very seriously.

It was because of his passivity and his fears of rejection, abandonment, and intimacy.

By the way, he tried my suggestion the very next week. "We got up off the couch ten minutes after doing what you suggested. She looked at me and said, 'Who are you?' Before I could answer she laughed and said, 'Never mind, I like this,' and we got up and got in bed and made love for the first time in a year."

This same man devoted an exorbitant amount of time to reading about relationships and marital counseling. He said he worked all the time on his marriage. But in reality, he thought his wife had the problem and not him.

Passivity then is an offense of omission—not

doing or saying what you need to, not responding, not accepting challenges, and refusing to take risks—rather than commission and that is one reason why it has been overlooked by clinicians and writers.

Passivity compels people to wait in a state of suspended animation until something or someone outside themselves "rescues" them from their current circumstances which would then allow them to have the full life that has been eluding them. This knight in shining armor (whether a person, the world, society or a supernatural being) is supposed to bring the passive person something they feel they have lost or had taken from them. That something could be hope, energy, love, trust, or faith. It could mean a perfect job, an unconditional lover, winning the lottery or having good parents. It is a psychological, physical, emotional, and spiritual condition that plagues even the most educated and self-directed people and therefore the whole person must be addressed.

Passivity pushes people to replay the feelings and memories they've stored in their brains and bodies possibly for decades. One of those feelings is the feeling of "Not Having What We Really Want or Need."

Symptoms of Depression and Passivity

- Sadness that does not abate

  The passive person is often sad in part because they do not actively grieve their missed opportunities, sabotaged relationships, passed over for promotions and much more. When depression is not bio-chemical it is usually brought about by repressed and denied emotions that continually build into full-blown depression.

- Loss of interest in activities previously enjoyed

  When people feel like they are not going to succeed or have been told since a young age that they can't succeed, eventually they withdraw from social, sports, and recreational activities and become more and more sedentary.

- Unintentional weight gain or weight loss

  The more they withdraw, the more their weight becomes a problem, and the more their weight becomes a problem, the more they withdraw. Passivity is a real Catch-22. Comfort food—which is packed with calories and sugar—becomes increasingly important. Sugar is a contributing factor in depression and passivity.

- Difficulty sleeping, or continual oversleeping

  Insomnia plagues the passive person. As lethargy sets in, sugar intake increases, sleep cycles get out of whack. Many passive people find the only time they are comfortable is when they sleep and sleep and sleep.

- Energy loss

All of the above ends up in energy loss. They feel tired and drained and since energy is the key to active engaging of life, they feel life has abandoned them. The feelings of worthlessness increases, they become irritable and hard to be around. They lose interest in sex and become constant complainers with unexplained ailments and excuses as to why they cannot be more engaging.

Because those around the passive person eventually become frustrated with the passive person who usually has so much unrealized potential, they also become uninterested and eventually avoids the passive person. As Edrita Fried, author of the book, Active/Passive, points out, this includes the therapeutic community who withdraws from treatment and refers their clients to other clinicians.

The passive person who is depressed finally receives some help from non-therapy psychiatrists or personal physicians in the way of anti-depressants that mostly mask the real problem sometimes for decades.

If a person is living a *half-lived life,* not achieving, not engaging life, experiencing little or no success in career, relationship, or creative endeavors how could they not

be depressed. If the passive person is going to therapy
say one hour per week and taking a serotonin re-uptake
inhibitor once a day but are living their waking life
with a less than satisfying relationship, going to work
that holds little or no passion, wanting to be something
they feel forever alludes them, how could they not be
depressed by the passivity that plagues them?

Solving the Problem of Passivity

Passivity is the compulsion to pursue the opposite of what
we say we want. This compulsion left unidentified and dealt
with leaves us unfulfilled at best, sabotages success, and at
worst depressed, hopeless, and feeling victimized.

"I don't care. Whatever you want is fine with me."

"It is not the job I want but in this economy you really
can't be choosy."

"He's not perfect but I'm 35 years old. Nobody's perfect.
I'm sure we will grow into love."

"I'd love to write. I've always dreamed someday I'd write
but I have kids and a job. Not everybody gets their dreams to
come true. Maybe when I retire…"

"I can't believe what is going on in Washington these

days. They are all idiots and con men. But there's nothing an average Joe like me can do about it."

"Go ask your father. If he says yes, then it's okay."

"That's the way the cookie crumbles."

"It's just not in the cards."

"It's not God's will."

"I guess I'm just unlucky."

"Some people get all the breaks."

"It is what it is."

Does any of the above ring a bell? If they do you may have some areas in life where passivity rules your attitudes, behaviors, personality, and decisions. Perhaps you have settled for less than you felt you deserved, or you "adapted" to your present situation or relationship rather than changing them. Did you "cop out," give up, quit, and become hopeless and helpless feeling like you were a victim of fate rather than a creator of your own destiny?

Unfortunately, many people have developed a greater connection to loss and feeling less than; they settle for unfulfilling relationships or careers that never quite achieve their creative potentials. Surviving, rather than thriving has become the state that many of us are not only used to but are compelled to pursue.

As one highly successful surgeon said to me who was growing increasingly wary of settling, "I always feel I am half the husband, half the father, half the friend, and half the doctor I know I can be even though I'm considered to be very successful in my field."

I said, "It sounds like you are living *a half-lived life.*"

"Exactly! But I am 50 years old. I don't want to say this at 60 or 70. I want the second half of my life to be a much fuller, satisfying life, but I'm not sure how."

I'll tell you what I told him. By coming out of denial, identifying the parts of your life where passivity prevails, working with the origins of your passivity, becoming aware of the signs and behaviors, and acquiring new, but tried and tested tools, information and insights that will serve as solutions you can fully engage life, work, relationships, creativity, parenting, grand-parenting and much more.

Every Time You Say "YOU," You Will Pay

The rule for men and women's communication before, say the 70s and 80s, was to not talk much about anything. Then there was a huge communication advance – "When you say or do, I feel…" This was a great break from the silent treatment to be sure.

About 20 plus years ago I thought, "Why do I need to say, 'When you say this, I feel…' Why not just say what I feel?" In other words, tell my lover, partner, parent, friend, child –

"I feel…;" "I need…;" "I want;" "I hurt;" "I'm sad;" or "I'm angry."

My client said to me this morning that her husband is just not as romantic and amorous as she needs him to be. I said, "How did you tell him about this?"

"I said he made me angry."

I said, why not say, "I feel angry when I don't receive enough affection?"

The client said, "Well, I learned in couples' counseling to say to my husband, "When YOU don't make love to me often, I feel rejected, not sexy, not beautiful, and I need YOU to find me attractive."

"What did he say?" I asked. "Did you feel heard – really listened to?"

"Not at all! He got defensive and said in his harshest tone, 'Damn, baby, YOU know I find you attractive. I married you, and it just seems like YOU are just too needy sometimes."

So, this is how most arguments or fights go but don't really go anywhere.

"I'm going to tell YOU what you're doing, saying how you're wrong." Then he or she is going to tell YOU how YOU didn't say that right.

We tell the other person what they did wrong, right, or what you're feeling is not right, and then you tell him/her, and they tell you, and this is a four-hour marathon where at the end I don't know any more about YOU and YOU don't know any more about me – and I jokingly say, "This is too often called marriage?"

Every time you say the word, YOU, you will pay when you're having a conflict, confrontation, argument – everything you do has some weird failure in it."

There's something about the word YOU that triggers a person's defensiveness; their buttons get pushed, or worse case, they severely regress. They stop listening to what we're saying and start preparing a rebuttal. "You" throws many into flight, fight, or freeze.

Here's what I used to do before the above became clear. When I was upset, disappointed, annoyed, and even angry or hurt: "YOU need to stop saying…" or "Why don't YOU….?" "If only YOU would stop or start or, God forbid, get some damn therapy."

> *"…The truth is you turned away yourself,*
> *and decided to go into the dark alone.*
> *Now you are tangled up in others…"*

Kabir, translated by Robert Bly

How to Tell the Difference Between Anger and Rage

A woman called me the other day for help. When I asked her what the problem was, she didn't hesitate and said, "I am living with the angriest man in the world." I said, "Tell me how he expresses his anger?"

After four or five descriptive sentences I said, "I hate to interrupt, but everything you've said so far is rage." And she said, "What's the difference?"

Anger is about the "Here and Now;" it is an active response to issues and situations occurring at the present time. You feel anger because of what your boss said to you this morning or because your spouse incorrectly balanced the checkbook this week.

Rage is about the "There and Then;" it is about our past. Rage is a reaction to what your boss has said to you every morning for the last year. What you've stuffed and bottled up all this time, suddenly comes gushing out like a geyser. Likewise, rage occurs because the checkbook has gone unbalanced for two years, seemingly warranting a deafening silence to correct or punish your spouse's behavior.

WHAT IS HEALTHY ANGER?	WHAT IS RAGE/ UNHEALTHY ANGER?
A feeling	A reaction
A primary emotion	Stuffs or masks emotions
It is neither positive nor negative	It is negative and inappropriate
Anger is energy	Rage is exhausting
Meant to be given away	Meant to be given up
It doesn't hurt anyone	Hurts everyone involved
Anger clears the air	Clouds communication
It increases understanding	Adds to confusion
Helps communication	Increases conflicts and misunderstandings
Rights injustices and wrongs	An injustice and wrongs people further
It increases energy, intimacy, and peace of mind	Decreases energy in people, increases the distance between them and causes discord
Healing	Damaging
Contained and controlled until proper time, place, and person	Pervasive, out of control, and misdirected
About the present	About the past
About "Me"	About "You"

Anger lives in the present and so takes minutes to be felt and expressed. Rage sticks around because it is grounded in the past. Because anger lives in the present, it takes moments or minutes at the most to be felt and expressed. When Jerome's wife was late for a special luncheon they'd planned, Jerome said, "I'm angry. Now, I only have forty-five minutes left for lunch before I have to return for work. Let's eat and make the most of our time."

Rage lives in the past and takes a very long time because it is grounded in our personal life history, and once unleashed, the result is that no one wants to eat with anyone because no one has an appetite left. Sandy's now ex-boyfriend was chronically late; Sandy's response was, "I'm tired of you always putting everything before me. Didn't your mother teach you it is rude to keep people waiting? I got here on time. I can't see why you can't!" ...And she was just getting warmed up. Clearly, there was more than anger going on.

Rage is what constitutes most marathon arguments. You know the ones that begin at eight o' clock after dinner, after the kids are put to bed, and is still going strong at one in the morning until someone cries, "Uncle," and says, "Does anyone know the original point of this?" or attempts to just share some feelings.

Anger is about me and rage is about you. If I express anger, I am telling you about me. Anger is revealing. If I am raging, I'm telling the other person about them and thus I am concealing what I am really feeling and going through. What many people do when they rage is this: They tell the other person about them. What they didn't do and shouldn't have done; why what they said is wrong, crazy, sick, and messed up. When they finally finish their diatribe, then it's the other person's turn to tell the first person about them and how what they said doesn't apply, and that if they'd said it differently, maybe they could be heard, and if they'd only read more self-help books, they wouldn't have said it at all. After that, then it's the first speaker's turn again, and then the second, and we affectionately call this marriage, and then very often we call it adversity and grounds for divorce.

Rage has moved more people out of relationships than U-Haul. It shoves everyone out the door, out of lives, or out of business. Rage pushes everyone away because no one wants to be around it.

On the other hand, anger expressed in present time and in an appropriate manner, actually draws people to you. If a man says to his wife, "I'm angry and I need to talk," nine times out of ten the wife will respond with something like, "Okay, tell me more," or "I'm listening," or "What's going on?"

If an employee says to a fellow worker, "I'm angry about what went on in the staff meeting this morning," most fellow employees will say, "Tell me more," or "Let's talk about it this afternoon over a beer." In other words, if I do not rage at you, you have no reason to run—indeed anger can create the beginning of many productive dialogues and initiate problem solving.

Rage engenders defensiveness, distance, and the feeling of being in some kind of danger. It shows disrespect and disregard for both the speaker and the one pretending to listen. Anger shows appreciation and respect. If one's boss is angry and says so and follows that statement with something like, "...and I'd like for you to meet me for lunch so we can discuss the issue,"—this says I value you and our relationship enough to make some time and request that you make some time to resolve the issue at hand.

Rage basically says —in no uncertain terms— I do not value you or this relationship enough to warrant an expenditure of my time or energy to try to achieve resolution.

Anger is a response to injustice, rudeness, impoliteness, impoverishment, impudence, and abuse. Rage is a reaction to situations, circumstances, people, processes, and problems. Responses are generated by present stimuli. Reactions are a re-activation of one's history and memories about people, processes, and problems.

These rage reactions are almost always disproportionate to what is being said or done or not done or said to one's satisfaction. Angry responses are proportional to what is coming towards us or being taken away from us.

These reactive behaviors and actions warrant these types of reactions from others: "Where is all of this coming from…?" or "Why are you making a mountain out of a molehill?" In other words, the person might be angry at a pounds' worth, but is dumping a tons' worth of rage on them.

Rage incorporates statements like "You always," or, "You never." They often include ultimatums and threats. The one raging believes in a black and white mentality, all or nothing, or my way or the highway.

Anger uses words like, "sometimes," "occasionally," and "every now and then." Anger is comfortable with some gray areas.

Anger engages conflict and rage runs from it. The angry men or women are in essence saying I have a problem and I am seeking a solution. Rage says you have a problem and that's the problem—no solution in sight.

Anger says let's confront these divisive issues; rage says let's further divide. A CEO who attended one of my corporate anger presentations, stood up during my talk and said, "I never run from confrontations. I stand toe to toe with anyone. I get in their face no matter what I have to do or say to get my point across." The sturdy, sixty-year-old with a crew-cut haircut sat down with a satisfied look on his face.

I responded, "Does that include yelling, calling people names, and other like behaviors or actions?"

"Whatever it takes!" he replied.

These actions and behaviors often employed in conflicted situations are self-defeating. One reason is that many people (including the aforementioned CEO) are avoiding conflict, in spite of how things may appear on the surface. They hate confrontations because in the past this meant they felt defeated by their parents, coaches, teachers, ex-wives, or husbands.

But perhaps a more significant explanation for so much avoidance is that most people have not been taught how to do it with a win-win attitude. Instead, we're taught there can only be one winner or one loser – an approach grounded in rage.

When we realize that it is inappropriate actions and reactions that cover our emotions, a new freedom is developed to speak out our feelings without fear of retaliation and retribution. And now that our responses are proportional to people and circumstances, neither the speaker nor listener has anything to fear.

PASSIVE WORDS USED BY THE RAGING PERSON:

- You always _____.
- You never _____.

- Why can't you _____ ?
- If only you _____ .
- It's all your fault.
- Shame on you.
- You're lying.
- When are you going to _____ ?

Interruption Rage:
The Kind of Rage No One Has Talked About

"People who fly into a rage always make a bad landing."

Will Rogers

See the tiny toddler going to explore the dog in the neighbor's yard? Now listen to what she might have heard – best case – "Get back here young lady." Worse case from the very anxious or perhaps exhausted parent, "Don't you ever leave this yard, or you'll get a spanking." I can't believe spanking still happens, but that's another issue.

Toddlers to teens to adults, trying to go forward, trying to get somewhere, testing limits and boundaries all thwarted in time and space by well-intentioned adults. Even the police officer who pulls us over for speeding to our destination is good intentioned most of the time.

I call it "Interruption Rage." It takes many forms: you're in a hurry and the person in front of you at the grocery store says, "I forgot something" – interruption. You're dancing with your sweetheart and someone cuts in – interruption. You're finally going on the much-needed vacation and the flight has been cancelled or the ship is held at port for a germy interruption. Or perhaps you're speaking at a lecture, having a heart-to-heart, come to Jesus talk, and the would-be listener interrupts – you explode – "Stop interrupting me, damn-it!" or you just shut down.

These small and large interruptions are stored in our bodies and fester there sometimes for decades.

We as children or teens could not safely express the momentary anger at those who guard the gates, monitor the hallways, shuts the doors on our momentum going forward literally or figuratively. So, we return to our cribs crying or we fantasize our cars have machine guns mounted on the hood so we can use them to get the guy who cuts us off on the interstate. Thus, the mild-mannered, never-in-trouble accountant heading home at 5:15 on a Friday after staring non-stop at columns of numbers gets cut off one too many times. They floor their Prius, drive like crazy, cutting others off to catch up to the surrogate, over-anxious parent, teacher, partner. The disproportionally pissed-off accountant best case starts cursing and shooting the bird. Worse case gets the offender to pull over and one or both go to jail, and we call this Road Rage – my new term – Interruption Rage!

How about you? Been interrupted recently?

"He piled upon the whale's white hump the sum of all the general rage ... and then, as if his chest had been a mortar, he burst his hot heart's shell upon it."

Herman Melville

Solving the Anger Problem for Alcoholics, Addicts and Those Who Love Them

"Anger ventilated often hurries toward forgiveness; and concealed often hardens into revenge."

Edward Bulwer-Lytton

Have you ever loved an alcoholic or addict? Probably most reading this would answer, "Yes!"

Alcoholics and addicts (love, sex, porn, gambling, shopping, eating, etc.) are angry about a lot of different things:

- Growing up in an alcoholic's or addict's home

- Being poor
- Being rich
- Wrong shape, size, color
- Terrible education
- Bad, dysfunctional relationships
- Hating their jobs

The list could go on and on. The people who love us have to put up with abuse, bad moods, depression, frustration, lies, manipulation, and lots and lots of broken promises and relapses.

Our loved ones pray for us, berate us, leave us, pay for interventions, give up on us, and come back to us or find another alcoholic or addict and experience the groundhog movie mania that can drive anyone insane.

Now one of the misleading missing pieces of recovery is the rule that you're not supposed to be angry. The Big Book of AA says we don't have the luxury of our basic human emotion – anger.

Years ago, I attended an AA speaker's meeting in Georgia. The guest speaker had 36 years of so-called sobriety. She was one of the angriest "old-timers" I'd ever listened to.

After the meeting about eight of us went to lunch. I was hesitant to say anything at first. Most of my lunch companions knew I worked in the field of recovery, and I have done so for 35 years.

Finally, Stan, who doesn't talk at the meetings said, "Did anybody think she was very angry?"

Well, the gossip flew around the table like buzzards pecking over a dead carcass. By the way, gossiping in my book, **The Missing Peace**, is a form of anger and rage. I slipped. But everyone at the table agreed she was pretty much full of venom that spewed out on all who heard her – so it wasn't just me. Never mind the alcoholic cliché, "If you spot it, you got it." Anger and rage are like a virus that spreads contagion (sorry about the timing of these words).

So, here's what I did after that meeting. I went directly home, sat down, and wrote this book, **The Missing Peace.**

It is not anger that drives us to drink, drives away the people who love us, but RAGE! Rage is what us alcoholics and addicts must avoid for the fear of relapse and self-destruction. Rage is what covers our emotions. Rage covers sadness, loneliness, and sometimes even love.

Anger is an emotion that is God-given for us to feel, to stop injustice, abuse, and get us out of stuck places. Rage is a stuck place that alcoholics, addicts, and those who love us have known too well.

Anger as Punishment and Revenge

Alcoholics, addicts, and adult children of alcoholics don't get angry – they get even. One of the reasons adults have such a problem feeling and expressing their anger is because anger has forever been tied to punishment and revenge. People who are punished instead of disciplined tend to seek revenge and are angry, and the best way to extract a pound of flesh is to punish the actual or perceived offender. "You drink – I'll show you – I'll not sleep with you." "If you overreact – I'll get you back – I'll have an affair."

A few years ago, I was in the Asheville airport waiting to catch a flight back to Austin. I was standing close to a very elderly lady who was sitting hunched over in a wheelchair in front of her sixty-something-year-old daughter and son. She was silently weeping, and the son looked down at her and said in a voice loud enough for all around him to hear: "Mamma, we told you if you cried, we wouldn't let you come back to visit anymore."

Do you hear the rage and revenge in his statement?

"That's right mother. We told you that you can't cry," said the daughter.

Can't you just imagine that fifty-something years ago this mother probably said to her children, in some public

place: "If you don't stop this crying, I'm never going to…."
She punished them with a threat. They wait fifty years for
revenge, and no one is even consciously being malicious.

The Difference Between Discipline and Punishment

Unfortunately, children are punished, and they become,
using Alice Miller's words, "Prisoners of Childhood," the
original title of her important book later named, The Drama
of the Gifted Child. Punishment makes children, adults,
criminals, and animals, at the least, untrusting, and at most,
full of rage. It is capricious – not well thought-out and not
stated before the fact. Where punishment is handed out, you
might as well hand out the alcohol and drugs to make them
forget that they have no choice and that others have extreme
amounts of power over them.

One time I asked a room full of counselors, educators,
and law enforcers if they could tell me exactly what would
happen to someone caught in their state driving while under
the influence? A couple of them said, "They would go to jail,"
another one said, "They would lose their license to drive;"
two or three of them said they would have to pay a fine, but
several said, "It would depend on who they are, who they

know, if they could afford a high-priced attorney and sadly, what color they are. A poor person of color who doesn't know anyone gets punished differently than someone who is white and has lots of money or connections." Hear the meanness in this? How enraged is someone going to be?

Now here is what makes people less angry – it's called: Discipline is almost angelic compared to demonic punishment. Here's why: punishment is after the fact or the offense. Discipline is prior to the act or offense. Punishment takes away healthy choice making. Discipline teaches how to make healthy and mature choices.

Punishment says here are the consequences I, or we, feel like handing out today, and discipline says know beforehand what the consequences of your actions will be no matter how we feel or don't feel today.

If my home state of Texas had huge billboards on every road entering saying exactly what the consequences would be for driving under the influence, say—YOU WILL LOSE YOUR LICENSE, YOU WILL GO TO JAIL, YOU WILL PAY $10,999.00 IN FINES, AND WE WILL CUT OFF YOUR BIG TOE – many folks would "think before they drink" or they'd think, "Damn, if they're going to be so clear, I'll just go to Alabama were the law is still ambiguous as hell and take my chances over there."

It is the same with children and adolescents who are disciplined rather than punished. They just don't tend to be as angry and have to get even later with their guards – I mean parents and teachers – because they were told what would happen beforehand.

One time my stepdaughter, who was about thirteen at the time, came in one warm summer evening very late, having been with her girlfriends chatting and forgetting about the time. As soon as she came through the door, she looked at me in disgust and said, "I know, I'm busted for staying out so late." The anger at being punished many times by her real father was on her face as she prepared to get more.

"Did I tell you what would happen before you went out if you weren't in by 9 p.m.?" She looked at me like I was asking her a trick question. She sighed heavily as all teenagers do, "No you didn't." "Well, that's my job – to tell you beforehand the consequences so you can make choices. So, no you're not busted. However, if you decide to stay out late again tomorrow night, you won't attend the sleepover this weekend with your girlfriends." I'll never forget what she said: "That sounds fair." And it was.

Punishment takes no time and is fast and very often furious. Discipline takes time and forethought. Punishment creates rage, resentment, and the need for revenge and retribution. Discipline creates a sense of well-being and feeling that one is cared for. All the young and older children I've seen and spoken with, and all the adults, have incredibly angry stories about being punished, and almost no one had stories of being disciplined.

Here's a little sidebar to all of this. The only institution that at least tries to practice discipline is – would you believe – the military. They have huge books of rules and regulations – if you go A.W.O.L. this, this, and this will happen. If you disregard a direct order – this, this, and this will happen. It is spelled out beforehand. You can actually look up what is going to happen should you violate the rules.

The bottom line – if you want to produce less angry children, who become less angry adolescents, who will then become less angry adults that feel safe, loved, and valued in this world, learn to discipline instead of punishing.

Angry adults need to drink and drug to forget how punishment caused them NOT to feel safe, loved, and valued in this world. Punishment just royally pisses everyone off, and then out roll the resentments, and out rolls the beer and whiskey barrels that are, at first, a barrel of fun and laughter, but eventually become containers of poison that kill families, friendships, opportunities, and relationships of all kinds.

Fair Fighting: 7 Steps

Jenny and her husband George both said, "we never fight," like it was a good thing. We explored further why they didn't fight and found out that they didn't really know how to fight fair, so they all but gave themselves an emotional hernia trying not to. However, what they did do on the rare occasion they met with disagreement is give in immediately to the other's point of view and resented it silently for days, weeks, and even years.

Fair fighting is a must for a healthy relationship to exist, and those who do it well and employ the following guidelines, will increase their chances greatly of having a long and loving time together.

1. No laundry lists. The past must stay in the past. Fighting in a functional way consists of staying current with our issues and conflicts. Confrontations must be about what is happening in the present, i.e., what you are upset, angry, frustrated or hurt by what was said or done, not said, or done yesterday, last night, this morning, etc. When people fight and keep referencing the past hurts, slights, a wound there is no way out of this verbal, emotional, and damaging cul-de-sac.

2. Abusive language must never be used. No one has the right to curse another regardless of the issue at hand.

While writing a letter expressing your anger and rage is acceptable, it must never be sent. Telling a friend or therapist about your issues and using strong language can even be advisable, but face to face, the language must not be abusive.

3. Putting agreed-upon limits on the fair fight is highly advisable. Example: Let's talk about this for thirty minutes, and if we have not reached an acceptable resolution, then we will take it back up tomorrow, and then following through with the agreement.

4. Getting rid of the word, "You." When most people disagree or argue they often pull out this word, cock it, and fire it straight at the heart of their loved one. "You" should, "You" ought to, why didn't "You?" "You" can't handle the truth, etc. The word "you" always creates defensiveness in the listener.

5. Use the word, "I." As I said before, "Intimacy begins with 'I'." In fair fighting I am going to tell you how I feel, what I think, what I need to change, what I want to happen.

6. Fair fighters never bring the other person's parents and their childhood into the discussion. This is off limits. I can tell my partner about my dysfunctional childhood, but I am to never tell her about hers unless she specifically asks for my take on them.

7. If you recognize that you are regressed and catch yourself before doing too much damage, you take a time out and "grow yourself backup" (see my book **Growing Yourself Back Up: Understanding Emotional Regression**), and then come back to the subject at hand thinking, speaking, and acting like a mature adult. Many men and women are conflict-avoidant because they do not know how to express anger and hurt in a functional way so they gunnysack, stuff, swallow, or repress until they explode or implode. Learning how to express anger appropriately increases the likelihood you will be heard and thus arrive at a solution to the distress.

Surrendering to What Is: Staying Open to What Will Be

*"You must give up the life you planned
in order to have the life that is waiting for you."*

Joseph Campbell

Yes, I know. You read the word; heard the word "surrender" and you think, not me, I'm not giving up. I won't accept defeat.

I've been thinking about this word a lot lately having just

sold my cabin in the Appalachian Mountains that I've had for 30 years and recovering from a hip replacement – letting the old hip go and getting a knee replacement next month. Lots of letting go.

But even earlier I remember the Christian hymn being sung in the old wooden Baptist church we attended on Sand Mountain in Alabama – the one I was baptized in at nine.

The old folks would sing:

...I surrender all,
I surrender all.
All to thee, my blessed Savior,
I surrender all...

I didn't really know what they meant. I didn't have a whole lot to surrender, give up, or give into – a Daisy BB gun shooting sparrows off the wire and the Johnny Cash album I got the same year for Christmas.

However, at the tender young age of 69, I find myself more than ever exploring this whole surrendering process, and I have more than a few clients trying to find ways to circumvent surrendering to what is in their lives.

I want to be clear; I'm not talking about surrendering to religion or God or Jesus or a Guru. I'm talking about letting go. Grieving what was, what will never be again, and feeling freer than ever to proceed into the present. I don't know anything much, but I do know the word religion means "to bind." So many of us are bound to our past, and Lord knows there's days I wish I had my cabin back, my energy of my 30s and 40s, and a lover or two long gone and the money I casually and foolishly let fly.

Most mornings now I wake up, have my morning coffee meditation, and begin again to surrender to the way things are. I take a few deep breaths, gently relaxing and proceeding to keep learning and feeling trust that I'm right where I'm supposed to be. I get up, work on a book that few people will probably read, counsel a few folks though fewer and fewer, check my mail, walk my dogs, and at night dream dreams of people, projects, and possibilities of days gone by.

One of my dear clients in her 60s said in session yesterday, "But I want back the fire in my belly that I used to have for my work. I want it to blaze again."

I could only empathize, but quoted a poem to her:

> *"... I thought my fire was out,*
> *I stirred the ashes*
> *I burnt my fingers."*
> Antonio Machado

Insane for the Light

I always wanted more quiet in my house as a child. By the time I was nine, I was seeking silence in the woods that backed up to the dirt-poor farm my dad bought. I'd sit on the million's old rocks on Sand Mountain in Alabama and let the wind and noiselessness wash over me and baptize me with serenity.

For 30 years I had a quiet cabin in the foothills of the southern Appalachians. I tell you all this because my home here in Austin, Texas, thanks to this virus being passed around like an inhuman hot potato, is quieter than it has been in a hundred years or more.

What do we do with the potentially deadly lull in assaults to our overstimulated ears?

Maybe, just maybe, we let more light into our daily lives – perhaps some almost heavenly light. We've been looking at modernity's electric lights, neon signs, cell phones and computer lights for so long that we have, to quote an old song, been "blinded by the light."

We have been Plato's cave dwellers for so long seeing dollar signs, credit cards, GNP flashing upon a movie-like screen in our collective caves. Chained to the dark floor thinking that what we are seeing projected on the screen is reality.

We may be the generations who break free of our chains, crawl out of the caverns, see the sun, and finally see that what we have been looking at is not real but illusions and brain-washed fantasies. Perhaps due to the Corona Virus (not "Chinese Virus") even in the quiet nights we can feel human again and:

"We know the road; as the moonlight
Lights everything, so on a night like this,
The road goes on ahead, it is all clear."

Robert Bly

And the road ahead, while cluttered a bit with hoarders and dishonest politicians, is also filled by those who are helping others, shopping for others, praying for others, loving strangers, and maybe, just maybe, we will start crawling out of the darkness of greediness and entitlement and live more gently on the earth and with each other so that when the Spanish poet, Antonio Machado, asks us the question: "What have you done with the garden that was entrusted to you?" We will say we tended it with lots more love and very timely tenderness.

"I am not a mechanism, an assembly of various sections..."

D.H. Lawrence

"Why?" The Most Useless Question

Yesterday during an intensive session with a client, he said, "Why did she leave me? Why didn't I see the red flags?"

Today during a phone session with a man in his late 60s, he said, "I've always asked myself why did I get to come back from Vietnam and so many of my buddies didn't?"

Some of my "Why's" include: "Why did my father become an alcoholic? Why did I?" and "Why did God/He/She/It make man's best friend the dog get so few years to live when whales and parrots and elephants get to be 50 and 60 years old and you can't take any of them for a walk in the park?"

There are 10,000 answers to every "Why?" we could ask, and none of them will really give us the peace "...that passeth all understanding..." as the Bible says.

The question, "Why?" can take up lots of wasted time and energy and get us humans to use so much of our allotted time on earth looking for the answers.

Ah! But "How?" Now that's a question worth devoting a lifetime to answering. How do we survive a divorce, a death, a longing? How do we heal and recover from alcoholism or being born into the family disease? How, as Stevie Nicks once sang, "...can the child within my heart rise above? ... can I handle the seasons of my life...?" "How" can be taught and modeled for us; experiences, strengths and hopes can be shared among us.

But I have to tell you the truth, I still find myself in the deep, dark, empty well of "Why?" But I don't stay there nearly as long as I used to.

I wish I knew what to tell you regarding why the things that hurt you, lost you, or found you occurred. However, I will keep encouraging and supporting you no matter how smart you are, jump into the oasis of "How?" and drink the cool waters of life.

> *"...Be patient toward all that is unsolved*
> *and try to love the questions themselves...*
> *Do not now seek the answers..."*
> Rilke, *Letters to a Young Poet*

Stop Pursuing Happy

The post-modern novelist Walk Percy says, "Anxiety summons us to an authentic experience," and if I strip down to all that I have learned, felt, seen, and heard then one way to move out of despair and anxiety is to stop the frantic and exhausting pursuit of happiness.

"The purpose of life is not to be happy.
It is to be useful, to be honorable, to be compassionate,
to have it make some difference that you have lived and
lived well."
Ralph Waldo Emerson

Coming here to this cottage in the woods I assigned myself what I know now to be an impossible task and that was to learn how to be alone again. I needed to know that in this rural setting with no lovers, wives, little money, but dump truck loads of peace and quiet if I could I acquire this illusory thing called happiness that everyone including me has been so desperately searching for most of our lives.

It turns out that once again the philosopher Kierkegaard would have a useful insight, "Happiness is the greatest hiding place for despair." "But Herr K" I whined, "the United States' Constitution says, as does the internet, formerly Madison Avenue everyman has the right to pursue happiness—it is a guaranteed if I get the right job, right education, right spouse, right kids, right house in the right neighborhood I should be happy right?"

So, happiness is "If this—Then." If I don't get the "right" everything then I'm not going to be happy. This is the cracked foundation on which our "happiness" home is built. It may take years or even decades or a divorce or a death for us to realize this house of straw could be blown over by the big bad wolf of bad luck, bad timing, and bad choices.

Yet it is in this house that we try to "make" our wives, children, husbands, or parents happy. What happens when happiness is not achieved or acquired, caught, trapped, and claimed as one's birthright? Most of us feel like we've done something wrong, missed the proverbial boat and maybe even fallen out of God's graces.

Outer circumstances, objectionable people, wars, bankruptcy, poverty, alcoholism seem to be the unhappiness rain that falls on both the just and the unjust. Happiness is more like a mirage in the desert that looks like a place we can eventually get to, claim as our own and drink its eternal, flowing waters—our own personal, emotional, spiritual, and financial oasis.

My house here in Southern Appalachia is surround by woods.

Clarissa Pinkola Estes says, "Go out in the woods, go out. If you don't go out into the woods nothing will ever happen and your life will never begin."

Thoreau said, "I went to the woods because I wished to live deliberately, to front the essential facts of life, and see if I could learn what it had to teach, and not, when I came to die, discover that I had not lived." Let me be clear here I am no Thoreau. I have Wi-Fi, laptop, desktop, iPad, iPhone, and a satellite tv with a million channels. However, what I've found now that I've lived here a year is that when I'm calm enough to remember to take full deep breaths and stand on my studio's deck and look at the gentle pastures, slopes and hills and I see the horses in the pasture across the road buck at the first sign of cool fall air I experience joy. When I'm quiet and not missing somebody or something and the geese fly right over my house every year about this time headed south, I feel a deep and abiding sense of peace and joy. When these honking angels decide to light on the still, small pond beside my studio, I think this joy could last ten thousand years in this one eternal moment.

Joy is something, as alone, lonely, sad, as I am almost every day, I can experience a dozen to a hundred times a day. While happiness seems like a permanent commodity, I should have bought off the internet and that I've paid for emotionally, educationally, and financially it always seems to be just beyond the grasp of these too short arms.

Happiness is pursued while joy is received. All these elegant trees on my property and the neighbors' stand waiting for the joy of their beauty to reach my eyes and then my heart. Sometimes when the wind is strong enough, they wave at me to get my divided attention. The pines especially today are insistent on saying hello. It seems like joy is enhanced in a direction proportion to how I reduce my expectancy and search for happiness. Joy can be experienced only in the precious moment. It can give birth to ecstasy, enthusiasm, and even momentary enlightenment. For us to be happy something has to happen to make us so. While joy is quixotic, mercurial, and temporary it is available anytime night or day.

Happiness then says something must change and you'll have me. Joy says you can have me anytime you want; I'm at your beck and call. Anytime you want to see that hawk that just flew over your head, that look in your own eye when you see your children that comes from within, anytime you access that ability you have to stop wanting, wanting things to be different than they are, wanting yourself to be different than you are, wanting happiness, you can experience the joy that is in you, and around you twenty-four seven whether you're in the woods or in a high rise.

"...I don't mind you saying I'll die soon, even in the sound of the word soon I hear the word, you which begins every sentence of joy...Ah, you're a thief the judge said, 'let's see your hands.' I showed him my callous hand in court. My sentence is a thousand years of joy."

Robert Bly

The Big Hope

Hope is the big brother to happiness who can bully the joy right out of us. Hope is the religious hole that was dug for many of us even before birth. "I hope it is a boy." "I hope it is a girl." We all hope whatever the gender that the baby is healthy. Then on the heartbreak occasion that the baby is not healthy, stillborn, where does the hope go? I fell into the hope well, as did my former wife with each successive miscarriage—four to be exact. Way before that I hoped my dad would stop drinking a million years ago now. I hoped I'd marry Phyllis. I hoped and hoped and splashed around until I almost drowned in the world's darkest wishing well.

Hope is a well-set bear trap that we set for others almost daily. The poet Rumi says, *"I shoot an arrow to the left, it lands right. I go after a deer and get chased by a wart hog. I dig a pit to trap others. I should be suspicious of what I want."* We provide even the people we love with just enough false hope or encouragement on towards the impossible outcome. Hope, like happiness is a turtle trying to catch and pass the hare of our desires. Hope is always in pursuit of something; being some other way than the way it is.

The Indian poet Kabir said it this way: "… now you are

tangled up in others and forgotten what you once knew and that is why everything you do has some weird failure in it."

So, we hope instead of have faith and wonder why love is so elusive in our lives and why "love" fails so often. One out of two marriages will end in divorce. Again, the culprit is the searching, the scanning the crowds, looking for the lover out there hoping they are looking for us. Rumi said, "The minute I heard my first love story I went looking for you, not knowing how blind that was. Lovers don't finally meet somewhere; they've been in each other all along."

Hope is what keeps me from grieving what I once had hoping it will come back. Hope puts what we never had in a small box, wrapped, and placed on the mantle above my fireplace. But it is this very grief work that "sorrow sweeps clean the house so joy may move in," says the Persian poet.

Now put your hope in the wish for your prince to come and if he or she does then you'll be happy. But when the mailman brings you the certified letter from the Prince saying "he is unavoidably detained and will not make it this lifetime" you're right back in dark woods of despair. Burn the letter and the envelope it came in and let Faith turn all our heavy lead hearts through the alchemical fire into the pure gold of love.

Faith is not necessarily tied to religion or spirituality. I'm talking about a secular kind of faith.

"I keep pursuing Faith, if for no other reason than because it is the place in our life that keeps reminding us of the necessity of Love – Not the romantic love of the poets, but the practical love."

Krista Tippett, *Speaking of Faith*

I can't tell you all that I have hoped for here on this mountain this year. Somewhere along the way, perhaps walking my three animal companions through the woods on a winter afternoon I began filling the hole in my soul with Faith. I've learned a few important things, perhaps six, but still remember this one and that is by letting go of hoping and holding the hands of faith and resting in the palm of process it will cure some of the sores of Despair.

Now here is my personal dilemma—more often than not I reside restlessly between hope and faith. I'm caught between a spiritual rock and a psychological hard place. For me, many days it feels like I'm asking myself to turn loose of a lifeline (oh we think this will be a best-seller; oh, surely you and your former wife will get back together, etc. etc.) tied to the back of the ship I just fell overboard. I want to reach out to hope and let it drag me back on deck. I hope the lifeline will be a woman who might turn and give my gray beard a second look or that God might throw one glance my way.

Faith whispers in my all but deaf ear, "you'll get a best-seller once your ego doesn't need one for artificial adulation that you still crave. You're less vain self won't care because you have faith and just keep writing like you tell all your students for the pure joy in it. As for hoping for more money which you spend an inordinate amount of time fantasizing about, you'll finally understand the mysterious words of your friend's poem, "animals give up all their money each year," and you'll remember the sparrows and the lilies of the fields. As for a woman coming into your life, perhaps not a lover, but one of the best friends you've ever had come your way without one ounce of effort on your part."

Faith is something I am incapable of acquiring like stocks or bonds or books from Amazon. Faith is accessed and generated from the inside out. Faith is an act of Grace where I let the wind blow, the sea be still or turbulent all the while accepting people, things, situations, comings, and yes goings, and even myself just as I am and allows me to "Know" – not believe that I don't have: "…to be good. You do not have to walk on your knees for a hundred miles through the desert repenting…" says Mary Oliver.

Secular faith comes down to this: "It will work out – it always has. Things have a way in the end to be just what we needed."

But my fear's screaming voice is so loud a deaf man could hear it say, "Don't listen to this shallow, sensitive voice of Faith's; she is a deranged bear wandering in the woods of philosophy and theology and does not serve your best interests like I do. Listen to your "Happiness" psychologist, mindful of your New Age body worker/guru. They will shed light on this whole matter and get you the gifts your body and soul crave.

Fear will talk your ear off and the little faith we have right out of us especially if something doesn't work out the way it should—a marriage, a promotion, an inheritance. I have listened to this voice so much during my life. I was afraid to leave my family, afraid to leave my hometown, afraid to leave the steady job in a retail clothing store in a windowless mall, afraid I won't make enough money to pay my bills if I follow my passions, my purpose and yes even my pain. I was afraid then to go to college, afraid I couldn't get my doctorate, afraid I could end up a sterile professor longing after the youth of new students each year to round out my dull routine of a life. I was afraid that my wife would leave, afraid I'd never be with another woman again, afraid I couldn't get it up again if I—afraid I'd get sick and become a burden to someone, afraid I'd actually die before I knew real faith and afraid that I'll keep forgetting that "perfect love casts out fear."

Saying Goodbye to Our Different Stages of Life

The young person's task is to primarily emancipate from his or her original family. I have a chapter in my book, **Recovery: Plain and Simple**, titled, "Saying Goodbye to Mom and Dad." The teen and early twenties, and now, even men and women in their early thirties, focus on establishing themselves in the world, and perhaps, creating a new family. The middle-aged person's task is to discover and express their own uniqueness as an individual and to more fully develop, expand their personality, which Carl Jung defined as, "the supreme realization of the innate idiosyncrasy of a living being." He also says, "the first half of life is to form an ego. The second half is to destroy it." In other words, really start the unbecoming process, the cookie-cutter, programmed, indoctrinated human we've become. We start dropping the false selves, and stop straying too far afield from the path, which Nature/God/Higher Power intended us to follow and become the person we were meant to be all along.

In the process of becoming a husband, wife, lawyer, teacher, millionaire, starving artist, and thus be able to meet the demands of careers and families, we end up abandoning pursuits and interests, which at one time in our lives, gave us enthusiasm, zest and meaning. In my book **The**

Half-Lived Life: Overcoming Passivity and Rediscovering Our Authentic Self, I encourage my readers, clients, and workshop participants to recall what their passions, talents and loves – before the bills and the babies, the mortgages and manias came – and turn and rediscover those all-but-forgotten and neglected sides of themselves. When they do, so many turn once again to music, painting, writing, poetry, drama, and other pursuits that enthralled them. Once this happens, our center of gravity of our personality shifts into action, and this center might be called our "Authentic Self," which is more capable of joy than our false selves are capable of attaining happiness.

By stripping away these personas during the Unbecoming process we come home to ourselves; we more deeply accept ourselves, and thus, begin to accept life on life's terms. Some might even go so far to say they "made their peace with their God," or "it's the way life is." We become a more receptive human being instead of a "human doing" and increase our ability to be less clingy to whatever comes and goes, surrendering what is no longer ours to hold on to and receiving that which is ready to come. We stop trying to force everything to bend to our will and stop thinking we know how everything, and everyone should go and who should come back and when. All of this creates a greater ability to exist in the "now." Once we stop turning the dials and pulling all of life's levers, we meet the great giver of joy – our deepest Self.

I'm Not Your Mother and I'm Not Your Father: How We Speak to Adults

"...all spoke the same language.
That was the time when words were like magic..."

Inuit

If you are not my parent, why do I feel like a child?

Growing up in Alabama, or at least trying to, my mother almost always talked to my dad as if he were her son or her father. Dad most often interacted with my mother like she was his daughter or his mother.

The language, tone, and style never (or almost never) were adult to adult. Now, I'm not the only Alabama man who had this unequal, paternal and maternal mode set in stone by the time I came out of the womb but mastered it shortly thereafter.

"Why did you leave your clothes on the floor?"
"When are you going into therapy?"
"No matter how many times I tell you..."

"You should call your parents."

"Why do you let the garbage or the bills pile up before attending to them?"

Folks these are statements and others like them that suggest they are being spoken to like a child or an unruly adolescent, but men and women – intelligent, well-educated adults – speak to each other this way on a daily basis.

"You're not going to work dressed like that are you?"

"Honey, you need to change your dress because it's too revealing."

I think you get my drift. Well, some couples are drowning in this sea of unsolicited criticism and all the while not exactly knowing a better way because we've been talking like this and hearing others talk down to or up to but never unilaterally, respectfully, and balanced.

I've been studying, reading, learning, and practicing a better way of communicating for over 35 years and I still slip as I'm sure most of you do.

We all must remember as often as we can to try and speak this almost foreign language called "adult-to-adult."

"Moment by moment, things are losing their hardness; now even my body lets the light through."

Virginia Woolf

Feelings Are as Important as Facts

First things first—A feeling is a fact at the moment a person is experiencing it. Emotion is as important as logic. In other words, if a person feels sad because their pet of ten years is lost or died, the sadness is as real as the sun and they are not to be talked out of their feelings but instead receive empathy. If someone is angry about losing a job, their anger is as real to them as the stars in the sky. Again, empathy is the main element in the emotionally intelligent person's repertoire of responses.

Unfortunately, many people, especially many men, have been taught that the expression of feelings and emotions makes them weak or inferior in some way. This is changing rapidly for younger generations who are being exposed to and supported in learning about emotional intelligence early on in their education.

Now no matter your age, I.Q., vocation, occupation, or education, you too hold in your hands a practical, easy to understand and implement, guide to increasing and enhancing your emotional intelligence, which will allow you to be more emotionally present and available to those you love, care about, and even work with.

The Loneliness Emergency: From Isolation to Connection

"...Loneliness can be a prison,
a place from which we look out at
a world we cannot inhabit..."

Poet David Whyte

Some people are on the mountain of loneliness—rock stars, chefs, and business tycoons. Some, who we will never know their names, are in despair, depression, and stuck, barely able to walk or stand. Sadly, these folks, like myself, used alcohol, and other addictions to numb the pain. Others finally decide that suicide is their only option to get out of their lonesome valley once and for all.

These are the people in W. H. Auden's poem, "The Unknown Citizen," written in 1939 and is perhaps even more relevant today.

"...he had everything necessary to the modern man, a photograph, a radio, a car, and a Frigidaire... Was he free? Was he happy? The question is absurd: Had anything been wrong, we should have certainly heard."

There is a loneliness emergency, and as the Beatles asked a long time ago, "all the lonely people, where do they all come from?" Some or most of them never make it to the emergency room or a doctor or therapist. And yet loneliness is a serious health risk. It is a predictor of premature death and is a bigger risk factor than obesity and the equivalent of smoking up to 15 packs of cigarettes a day according to recent studies.

In 2018 we have 500 channels, computers, 80% of the world's population have smartphones that they can talk on, watch TV on, listen to music and soon driverless cars and yet, 50% of Americans report regularly feeling lonely and one study shows those between 16-24 are the most likely of any age group to report feeling lonely.

There is a loneliness emergency in this country and others. I finally came out on the other side of the deepest, bone-lonely period of my life after my divorce, so I'll be saying more about this emergency, but for now, touch a friend, call, hold someone, speak to someone face-to-face, and for God's sake, if you are suffering from loneliness tell someone about it.

Letting Your Feelings Out of the Cage

*"If you want to go fast, go alone.
If you want to go far, go together."*

African Proverb

A few months or a lifetime ago (virus months are like dog years), I wrote a blog on the loneliness epidemic.

Americans, in spite of technology, are some of the loneliest people in the world due to too many factors to go into (besides, you know most of them). However, this damn demonic disease called "Corona Virus" has increased the loneliness factor to the tenth power. The isolation for many who are in their homes almost full time has become unbearable.

At first blush with boredom in February and then March, I thought, as an introvert, it didn't seem like my life was much different than pre-virus times. However, March turned to April, "the cruelest month of all," and April turned into May, then June, and then July, and it became even deadlier. I realized that even though my body likes to stay at home, the forced loneliness and the all but choice-lessness loneliness was getting to me.

It has been too long since I shared caffeine or touched someone or been touched. Pre-virus all my friends, and most of my clients, get and give an unmasked hello and goodbye hug. Most of you reading this (if you've gotten this far with my blog-rant) can see the irony given the power of human touch to heal and release endorphins has been researched, recorded, and now removed from everyday life.

Now we all know we can be lonely in a crowd or even

in a family. Some people are getting a little testy from sheltering in place and are going crazy for some solitude. The apartments, condos, and even mansions are getting a little too small for some.

Whatever kind of loneliness you might be experiencing, please remember impatience, boredom, nausea, and anger, are all under the umbrella of the virus, and though our fearful leader says it will "one day magically disappear," it's not, at least for some time to come. So, try not to make any big decisions, moves, or messes.

This is the time for extreme radical tenderness and compassion with yourself or with those you are staying at home with for the near future. And keep reaching out any way you can – through emails, texts, video chats, remember letters and cards, and for God's sake, share your feelings of fear and exhaustion with your cabin fever. As James Taylor said, "tell somebody the way that you feel;" and just maybe you'll feel it beginning to ease.

Isn't It Touching?

Most men are touch starved, touch phobic or sexualize a tender touch.

Many men have never availed themselves to a therapeutic massage by males or females. I was one of those men into my 30s. The first time I received a healing massage, I wept and wondered why I'd waited so long and why I had to pay $30 (back then) for human touch when lots of people got it for free.

To be hugged by a man was taboo in the Deep South of my raising. Real men shook hands. Some of us eventually graduated and upgraded to what I call the "Heterosexual A-Frame Hug." This is a leaning, barely touching, beating the hell out of each other's backs, for no longer than 1 ½ seconds.

You see many men that I grew up with were, and some are still, "Homophobic." This term has lost its true meaning. The word does not mean fear of gay people; it means: Homo = Man, Phobic = fear – fear of men – the competition, bullying, beatings, cheating, lied to, molested, and abused by fathers, uncles, priests, etc.

So, all this has led to men not only alienated from men but isolated and lonely in their own bodies. Perhaps this is one of the many reasons that men die earlier than women and are lonely to their core and ultimately leads to a breakdown of male friendships and male non-sexual intimacy, the lack of mentors, and the fear of being held in general, which after thousands of hours of therapy and men's work a lot of us finally receive a safe man's embrace.

Here is an excerpt from Canadian poet, Alden Nowland:

"He Sits Down on the Floor for the School of the Retarded"

> *...It's what we all want, in the end,*
> *to be held, merely to be held,*
> *to be kissed, (not necessarily with the lips,*
> *for every touching is a kind of kiss).*
> *Yes, it's what we want, in the end...*

So, What's the Holdup on Being Held?

As Part II to "Isn't It Touching," I thought touch-starved men might be interested in considering the following ideas.

1. Most men either have one male friend who lives in Russia or Tasmania, but they haven't met face to face in 30 years, or they have none – solution? Get more men in your life.

2. Where to go to get a healthy male hug or simply to be held? Men's gatherings like the one I led two weeks ago in the mountains of North Georgia – 70 good men with Mentor Discover Inspire (MDI)! 12-Step Programs that sober men attend. Go to a Mankind Weekend – an excellent place for male comradery.

3. Stop settling for bullshit conversations sometimes, not always, but talk and listen to what is going on inside of them and you.

4. Deal with the "Moral Injury" perpetrated on you by boys and men and the hurt and injury we have done to other men. (Definition of Moral Injury: An injury, a wound to an individual's moral conscience and compass when men witness or fail to prevent acts that go against deeply held codes of conduct. Moral injury is a betrayal of what's right and often results in PTSD because of unprocessed grief, guilt, anger, embarrassment and shame.)

5. Remember C.G. Jung's words, "Condemnation does not liberate, it oppresses." So, don't condemn men who need to be touched, and for God's sake, don't condemn yourself for still being a live, breathing, touch-starved man.

I Lost Myself

"...the wind left. And I wept. And I said to myself:
what have you done with the garden
that was entrusted to you?"

Antonio Machado

Most people never really know the date, time, or place that we let ourselves slip out of sight.

I know when I got my genetically pre-dispositioned heart attack several years ago that's when I saw myself "slip out the back Jack," and a few years later after a couple of knee replacements and a hip replaced, (God, I'm old!) and entering semi-retirement, there wasn't a whole lot of me left in the last couple of years of my sixteen-year marriage.

I can't tell you how many women clients or workshop participants have said, "I lost myself in this relationship," and quite a few men have said the same thing.

In more than a few workshops and lectures I said the following:

How many of you ended a relationship, broke up, divorced and after the sobbing and grieving and anger work pulled yourself back together with friends or professional help? And then you started writing in your journal, joined a Yoga or Pilates class, meditated and/or prayed, planted a little garden, and felt better than you had in years?

And then you met this new, wonderful, personal growth lover or partner who kept nodding their head yes to every-thing you said – "I like coffee, you do too? I like movies, you do too?" You can even get a recovering redneck to say he likes the ballet, and then six months later you no longer wrote in your journal, quit going to Yoga class, and your garden was now a plot of weeds?

Damn! A lot of hands go up in the air as a symbol, "Me too! I did exactly what you just said."

So, if you've lost yourself or are seeing yourself beginning your own personal disappearing act, treat yourself as if you are your own best friend. Make a list of all the things you loved or still love to do. Tell your loved one if they are still with you what it was like in previous relationships and how you lost yourself and how you may be losing yourself in the present one. Ask your partner for support to hold on to yourself and still love and support them to do the same. Dust off that journal, recommit to yourself; get help if you need it from friends, coaches, and/or counselors. If you are in a relationship currently, here is the best remedy: slow down; get to know each other; court each other's soul; be friends first because friends don't tend to lose themselves.

Good luck.

"I am not I.
I am this one
walking beside me whom I do not see,
whom at times I manage to visit,

and whom at other times I forget;
who remains calm and silent while I talk..."

Juan Ramón Jiménez

Masculinity

Masculinity means so many different things depending on who you ask. In 1991 there was a meeting set up by Warren Farrell, one of the earliest pioneers in men's issues, at his mountain retreat in California. A dozen or so of us so-called leaders of the Men's Movement were invited to come and share our thoughts, feelings, and positions regarding the question of what true masculinity was, among other topics, including whether or not the Men's Movement should be politicized like the earlier Women's Movement.

By the way, this is where I got to be friends with poet Robert Bly. He and I shared a cabin together and it allowed us to start and continue a relationship as equals and colleagues for over 20 years. This relationship helped to forge my understanding of my own masculinity.

It is kind of ironic that the recognized Father of the Men's Movement was a character like Robert Bly. He is one of the most sensitive, kind, generous, and generative men I've had the pleasure to know, learn from, work beside and be friends with. It took a wild-haired bear of a man who is a poet and a master storyteller of fairytales and ancient fables to lead men right down into their well of pain. Here is a man who blends intelligence, emotion, music, poetry, passion, and love of all things into what would be considered a new definition of masculinity.

As for the question, should the Men's Movement be politicized, Robert and I, and a couple of other early pioneers, Shepherd Bliss and Aaron Kipnis, agreed that the Men's Movement should focus on an interior journey, not an exterior one. Women had to become political to assert their rights as equals in every way to the predominant male culture. Robert and I said, "We've been political; let's go into our souls, bodies, and hearts" for answers on how to live in the 20th and 21st centuries. Poetry – his own, Rumi's, Hafiz's, Machado's, Jimenez's, and dozens of others – was a way inward, and fairytales would help those of us who listened as he said – often accompanying himself on his Greek instrument, the bazuki – "We're leaving our time now."

One of the main reasons I was asked to attend this little-known conference was due to my approach to masculinity. I felt, believed, and taught through workshops and writing that men who are abusing alcohol, anger, rage, and drugs should sober up and discover who they really are under all the layers of addictions.

Both Robert and I are adult children of alcoholics which greatly impeded our growth and development of our masculinity; we talked about this and other issues while we shared that cabin and for 20 years after.

So, what is masculinity? I can tell you much more easily what it is NOT:

True masculinity is not John Wayne movies.
True masculinity is not who has the biggest cock or stock options.
True masculinity is not homophobic, xenophobic, anti-feminine or anti-feminist.
True masculinity is not full of rage.
True masculinity is not oppressive.
True masculinity is as tender as it is tough and tenacious.
True masculinity is a balance between the wild and the sensitive.
True masculinity is not afraid of being called names like prissy, pussy, or fags because we read, write poetry, play music, and sing to our brothers,' fathers,' and sons' souls.
True masculinity mentors the young men and women.
True masculinity weeps, mourns, celebrates, laughs, wonders, looks at how we were wounded and how we have wounded others and our planet.

I could go on, but the truth is that true or deep masculinity changes over time with new information and experiences and at different stages of life. It changes as the seasons of a man's life change. My own sense of masculinity at 69 is somewhat the same as it was at 35 but also much different. My masculinity now includes a kind of patience my younger masculine self-did not have with people, processes, and life in general. My masculinity incorporates the old Arabic saying, "Haste is of the devil, slowness is of God." My masculinity, while still a little competitive, doesn't do harm to other men. My masculinity finally learned lovemaking is 100 times better than fucking women I don't know hardly or at all. My masculinity sits on the porch much more often and drinks coffee and eats banana nut bread without worrying about calories. My masculinity demands I stay in shape, but my ego is not damaged if I don't, and as my old friend, Martín Prechtel, would say at our men's conferences, "Long life and honey in the heart."

Home for the Holidays

There's something about the season from Thanksgiving to New Year's that will bring out the adult children's worst fears and greatest expectations. One of the biggest fears is that we'll be alone. The biggest expectation is that we'll finally have a Christmas the way a normal family does. This Christmas we'll all be together, and we'll all love each other and communicate our feelings openly and honestly.

For years I started dreading the approaching Christmas season as early as June. With some work, I finally made it up to September or October before I went into pre-holiday depression. That's finally changed, but it's often still hard. There's still a little boy in me who wants to believe in Santa Claus and an overnight cure for alcoholism, dysfunction and co-dependency.

Many co-dependent adult children seem to feel absolutely compelled to go home during the holidays, no matter how much they don't really want to.

"Mary, are you going home for Christmas this year?" the therapist asks the Mary's and John's of the world.

"I don't want to. It's always terrible at our house. It's crazy. Mom works herself to death getting the meal prepared. Dad and my brothers stare at endless football games. There's always so much tension in the air you could cut it with a knife. No one really talks to each other and everyone acts like there's nothing wrong. I think I'm the only crazy one in the family because I either want to scream or run away and everyone else looks like everything is fine… Yes, I'm going home."

"How is it that you feel you must go if it's so bad?" Therapists who specialize in co-dependency already know but we ask anyway.

"Mom would be crushed if I didn't. Dad would be so upset. My sisters and brothers would disown me. And my parents always say, 'Grandma isn't going to be with us much longer and is dying to see you. If you can't think of us, at least think of her. Don't be so selfish!'"

So adult children go, and everything is pretty much like it's always been. They are so tense they say or hear something that sets things off and the whole holiday ends up a big mess. Hope that "this time would be different" gets postponed until the next Christmas. No one has a good time except the ones still in denial.

When adult children of dysfunctional families survive the holidays and return to their groups and private sessions, they have lots to work on. So, going home does give us therapists plenty to wrestle with from January to the middle of November. Many want three to six extra sessions per week after that if they can afford them. Most of us really just want someone to tell us we don't have to go home this Christmas if we don't want to. Going home can be for some the loneliest way to spend the holidays. We go to not be alone and yet loneliness was exactly what I would feel the most as I looked at the way our family really was.

As a footnote to all of this, when I didn't go home, I had

a tendency to isolate and white-knuckle my way through the holidays. Since I didn't feel I fit in anywhere, I'd often be by myself. People would ask me over for dinner or to come home with them and be a part of their family. I'd decline and go to a couple of movies on Thanksgiving, Christmas and New Year's Day. I always knew the best pictures to tell folks to see when they returned from visiting their families.

The bottom line is that no matter what I did to not feel alone—whether it was to muster up the wherewithal to go home or stay by myself—I still felt alone.

Last year I didn't do either. I went to Al-Anon and CoDA meetings during the holidays and felt for the first time that I was not alone. I fit in. All the meetings were made up of those of us who were ready to stop going home and pretending or enduring the ordeal. Yet we were not hiding out in movie theaters and under the covers in our bedrooms. It felt great. This year, after 30 years in recovery, the holidays were finally happy. But the year before? ... Well!

Grieving: The Doorway to Healing and to Maturity

During my 35 years of counseling and working with men and women, I have been asked so many times: "How do you grieve?" or "How do you begin grieving?"

Here are the five things necessary to do deep grief work around any change, transition, death, loss, break up, or divorce:

1. One needs an awareness that grief is the proper response to all loss, change and transition, and that it is a doorway into our maturity.

2. We need to devote as much time as it takes, letting no one tell us to move on or out faster than we are ready because as we know time is the great healer.

3. In order to do deep grief work, one must ritualize the process. These rituals move the pain and the sorrow up and out faster than a catch-as-catch-can approach to grief can ever achieve.

4. We need a community of supportive people as we go through these transitions and losses because grief is not to be done entirely alone but in a community.

5. Having navigated our way through the treacherous waters and shed our tears, we need to employ our community and have a celebration that says we came out on the other side.

Also, one of the seven stages of grief is anger, and the coming holidays can be a time when people feel angry about all kinds of different things. Additionally, it is a season when a lot of folks get depressed, anxious, family histories surface, and loneliness prevails.

✦

Third Act of Life

Scene 1

I'm an aging man sitting with his three dogs in a rented house way out of my price range. Divorced now for five and one-half years, I share custody with my ex of the Malamute, Benjie dog, and Baby Bella, the dachshund mix.

Now you folks reading this who are under 50, keep reading because you'll get here someday, and the 50 and over, let's talk about being relevant. We know we have a lot less life in front of us than we do behind us. But like the rearview mirror says, if you're still able to drive, "objects may appear closer than they really are" (or something like that).

Those objects are former careers, ex wives and husbands, grown children, large homes we've had to sell and have scaled down to smaller apartments, condos and tiny houses, some of you with your partner of over 25 years barely fit in those small spaces. Let's be honest – some of us have put on a little weight or at least I have.

If you are able to keep your house you spend an inordinate amount of time mowing the yard, weed eating around your fence or sidewalk or fixing something all the time whether it's broken or not. Perhaps you have a small garden or play 36 holes of golf every day when your aching joints or back will allow.

You retired prematurely instead of becoming re-inspired or re-imagined your future. Your pilot light went out or so you think. Well, hell let's reignite the damn thing! That's how we stay relevant.

How does one do that when life's matches are so hard to find and even some of those are moldy with age like some of us?

Scene 2

First, I had to accept my stage of life and the fact that I'm 69 even though in my head I think I'm 40 but with a really messed up body – damn arthritis. Second, I had to grieve the loss of my 40-year-old body which also includes my former devilish good looks and see my baby blues disappearing from sight. Third, and most importantly, I had to accept that I don't know how to do my Third Act and stop beating myself up for not knowing and begin to learn.

You folks just getting to your Second Act, or coming to an end of it, you're not supposed to know either – so cut yourself some slack and start asking us older folks – and that right there is a way we can stay relevant.

Scene 3

Here are a few ways to stay engaged and energized. If you wanted to be an actor but became a banker, go to your local community theatres, and try out or work backstage.

If you were a teacher, volunteer to teach inner-city youth or community college or a seniors' class at the assisted living facility. A carpenter can volunteer for Habitat for Humanity – a plumber, electrician – same. Policeman/woman, fire fighter, doctor, lawyer, or Indian Chief, help the poor and the homeless, write your memoirs, take classes in something you've always wanted to learn. Create, create, create a second career. Yes, I know you have Netflix, Amazon Prime, Hulu, Showtime, Sundance – go ahead and watch a movie now and then, but don't sit too long. As Einstein said, "A body in motion..." or as the poet Rumi says, "Let the beauty we love, be what we do. There are a thousand ways to kneel and kiss the ground."

I know for a fact that the Third Act is less than total fun, but since we're on this side of the grass, never stop asking the questions: "What do I love?" and "What is next?"

Seven Years to Seven Minutes

"It ain't dying I'm talking about, it's living..."

Gus in "Lonesome Dove"

Let's say your doctor tells you (God forbid), "You have seven years to live."

Here are the four questions I had to ask myself when I did this exercise:

1. Where will you go?
2. What will you do?
3. Who will you take with you?
4. What are you waiting on?

When I answered these questions at seven years, I said I'd live in my mountain cottage in the pigmy southern Appalachians and travel back and forth to Austin. I'd continue to write and see clients part-time and would take my then wife with me to both places.

Okay, now your doctor didn't read the x-ray report correctly and said, "Sorry, you only have seven months."

Then I answered the same four questions. I was surprised by how those answers changed. The answers really changed when it got to seven weeks and dramatically changed when told seven hours and then seven minutes.

Well, I did this exercise with a good man who came for a two-day Intensive Session with me at my mountain retreat. He had literally been told his cancer would take him in six to eight months.

Long story short – when I asked him the four questions with only seven months to live, he said: "I want to take all my old friends and family to the Redwood Forest in California and find a tree that we could make a circle around, lay down on the ground and hold hands."

What a beautiful image he placed in my head. I asked him the last of the four questions: "What are you waiting on?"

He replied: "That's asking an awful lot – the money for airline tickets, car rentals, etc., etc."

I'll come back to this in a moment.

His wife was with him and I asked her to come in the studio where I had a daybed.

I told him and her, "Now you only have seven minutes to live, and I'm going to step outside and give you your privacy."

I had no idea what would happen. When the time I'd set rang, I went back in and they were spooning, weeping, and laughing. The wife wiped away some tears and said, "He told me something he's never told me in 35 years of marriage."

I never asked what that was – it was theirs' only.

About a half-year later, his wife called me to tell me two things. The first was that he and she and 14 family and friends went to that magnificent forest, circled a tree, and held hands. Not one person he asked declined. The second thing was that he was peaceful, serene, and beautiful in the days before he went. He knew he was deeply loved."

I ask you to try the exercise and answer the four questions, and then answer this fifth question posed by one of the greatest poets, Mary Oliver:

> *"...Tell me, what is it you plan to do with your one wild and precious life."*

The Summer Day

What Now?
Thoughts and Poetic Direction

"When you come to a fork in the road, take it."

Yogi Berra

No matter what age you are or what stage of life you are in you will come to Berra's forks in the road. Most folks have four prongs pointing forward, none to the past unless you turn the fork on yourself and stick it in you to see if you're done.

People ask me all the time, "When will I be done?" My silly reply has always been the same, "Only steaks get done."

Alright you've lost a relationship, parent, career, your youth, or a home. I, by the way, have lost all of these the last couple of years and I've asked myself this question every day: "So what now?"

For many this question gets harder the older some of us get. But most of us are driven to seek out the answers anyway. Some of us go slowly and tease the answers out like pulling cotton from its stubborn boll or taking a pearl out of an oyster that doesn't want you to have the "great prize." Others attack the question like a bull in the china shop only to get hooked by our own horns – hooked on drugs or alcohol or other numbing processes to make us think we're really searching for the answers, but we're not.

To put all of this in a more poetic way, if we're not careful during these difficult times we may end up, to quote William Stafford, "following the wrong god home we may miss our star."

Perhaps you are having to do what I'm doing – drawing on the support of new and old friends, even though sometimes making contact using my 300-pound cell phone to call them when I'd rather pull my comforter over my head and go back to sleep. I've also enlisted the help of a new therapist – nope, I'm not done with therapy or 12-step meetings.

I also have to keep cultivating good crops of patience, something I don't grow very well because I want the answers to "What now?" "When?" Now, dam-it!

Then I re-read T.S. Eliot's words one more time:

"I said to my soul, be still and wait without hope, for hope would be hope for the wrong thing..."

Another thing I try to remember is to pay deep attention to my body and a little less to my mind – thank you T.S.

I recall the words of the Sufi poet Rumi: "Let the body speak openly now without your saying a word..."

And if I don't listen to my body during these tough transitional times and slow everything down, I will commit way too many errors in my impulsive decision making and end up like another of Rumi's poems:

"...I plot to get what I want
And end up in prison..."

So, I hope this short text, while not answering yours or my question: "What now?" provides a little comfort and some poetic pointers to the way forward.

You are not alone, and I'll give Rilke the last words for now: "Let everything happen to you: beauty and terror..." and "Be patient toward all that is unsolved in your heart and try to love the question..."

✦

And now for a break from psychology and into the realm of fairytales

*"We must let go of the life we planned,
so as to accept the one that is waiting for us."*

Joseph Campbell

…The King then decided to find his ugly snake son a bride and get him married so his golden-haired son could inherit the kingdom. So, he looked all around his kingdom for a suitable bride. He put an ad in the classifieds saying, "Single, slithery snake seeking life-long partner, not very good table manners and too many other bad habits to mention." You'd be surprised how many takers there were. Passive women come out in droves. Some women love snakes it seems, especially the tall, dark, and handsome, wounded ones, with lots of intensity and potential.

A beautiful bride was selected, and they had a wedding, and on the wedding night the snake ate his bride. Why? Because she was so poorly mothered that she didn't know what to do. She passively gave in to the snake's demands.

The King ran another ad and an unbelievable number

responded, and there was a wedding, and again the snake ate his bride on the wedding night. And so, it went with the third, fourth and fifth. The women of the kingdom began hearing about the snake's taste in women and they were getting a little harder to find.

However, there was a woodcutter's daughter who was extremely in touch with her own emotions, and anything but passive, decided to go for it. Unlike her predecessors she went to find The Wise Old Woman, which in fairy stories is code for "Good Mother." She lived in the woods – the same one who helped the Queen get pregnant – and asked her for advice. She gladly gave it but insisted that, unlike the Queen, she must follow her instructions to the letter, or she could also become snake food.

The Old Wise Woman told her to take her time and not rush into anything. The old woman told her to make seven beautiful wedding blouses (code for activeness and creativity) and wear them on her wedding night, and to take a bucket of sweet milk and a steel brush with her to the bedroom.

So, she took about a year making these blouses. Waiting makes impatient snakes hungry. Finally, on the wedding night the snake closed the door and was ready to have some wife food. But first he wanted a little pre-dinner show, so he said, "Take off your blouse."

"I'll take off my blouse if you will take off one of your

skins," she replied.

"Do what? You got to be kidding. That would hurt like hell. Besides, no one has ever asked me to do this before." So due to his hidden desire for real love he began taking off his skin and you should have heard the shrieks, cries, and yelling. You know it hurts to shed a skin. It also hurts to learn how to love. This snake had a lot to learn about how poorly he had loved in the past.

The woodcutter's daughter took off the blouse only to reveal another one under it. The snake looked perplexed and was beginning to get a little frustrated.

"Take off the blouse," He growled.

"I'll take off my blouse if you will take off your skin."

"I can't believe you're asking me to do all this stuff. Every woman I've eaten, I mean, loved has never asked me to do this before. What do you want from me? Emotional honesty, availability? What next? I suppose you want me to open up and tell you what I really feel?"

So once again you should have heard the moaning and groaning of the snake shedding another layer of skin. The woman removed a blouse only to reveal another one. Well, the snake was getting pretty irritated to say the least and was beginning to get the picture that this woman was not going to be as easy as the other brides, and that she knew how to take care of herself and ask for what she wanted and wouldn't settle for anything less than what she deserved.

How many times have we all settled for less than we truly wanted or even deserved?

Well to make an already long story short, this went on for seven times until finally there was nothing left of the snake except a little puddle of a former self lying on the floor.

That's what grieving and learning to really love will do to a snake or a man – reduce him to nothing and show him he knows nothing about mature relationships.

The bride took her bucket of sweet milk out from under the bed and dipped her steel brush into it and scrubbed what remained of the snake for about an hour or so. She loved him well. She prepared herself to love him well, and in so doing, prepared herself to be well loved.

The next morning the wedding chamber doors opened and out stepped a beautiful, stunning, Prince with his smart, respected bride, and they got the family together and had a great feast and lived happily ever after.

The snake didn't know the previous women he married and then ate. Carl Jung referred to these women as the "False Brides." The "True Bride" is the maiden with the seven blouses who took her time, who took care of herself, had great boundaries, and knew her limits, and demanded that the Snake/man mourn his losses, and that way he would truly know himself and her. The snake thought that he was simply a giant snake but there was so much more to him, and while the bride to be knew this, she was prudent and patient enough with him so that he found out just who his true self really was.

PART 2

REFLECTIONS FROM MY PREVIOUSLY
PUBLISHED WORKS

Writing from the Body: For Writers, Artists, and Dreamers Who Long to Free Their Voice

"Yet if I were asked to name the most important items
in a writer's makeup,
the things that shape his material and rush him
along the road
to where he wants to go, I could only warn him to
look to his zest, see to his gusto."
Ray Bradbury *Zen in the Art of Writing*

I've been teaching, coaching, and counseling new and
seasoned writers for over three decades. It has long been one
of my favorite things to do – to help writers get their words
whirling in their heads and on to the blank page. I know how
hard it can be. I wrote six drafts of the first chapter of my
best-selling book, **The Flying Boy: Healing the Wounded
Man**, before I got out the seventh one, which thank God it
worked. Why was it so hard? Because I couldn't get out of
my head. I couldn't stop imitating my favorite authors. I had
to come to terms with "who do I think I am to write a book?"

I couldn't get past the fear of what people I loved might think if I told the truth about my life. Now 23 books later—novel, poetry, self-help, memoirs, screen plays, non-fiction – it still can be hard, but I've helped more than a few writers and dreamers over the years because I've learned a few things like:

The call to write is a call that's received in the body first. If we are to answer the call, we have to feel every part of our lives. In order to write and write well we must get out of our heads. For everyone who is tired of living life in the little closet between the ears, answer the call to write, paint, sing, dance, etc.

A writer can't afford to walk numbly through the house with a blanket over the head. When the lover steps, dripping from the shower and bends to dry herself, the writer's eye takes in the droplets as they fall to the floor, and the fire of creativity is ignited: the little spheres of light encased in the water, the gently sloping curve from hairline to ankle, her hands as they guide the cloth over her skin. Let others drink life from a tiny cup! Face plunged in this ocean, the writer reaches deeply with every pore, not just to taste, but to merge with that greater Body, to experience the larger Self. To live like that, and to create from that truth, we have to radically reclaim and renew the body.

For hundreds of years poets and writers have described

the creative process as a physical urgency, a sense that things will fly apart if they don't get the pencil to the page in time. Creativity is not tidy or polite – it's insistent. It calls us to feel, not dimly, not safely, but wildly, passionately, in every cell and fiber.

I needed a lot of help to discover my own body of writing. Most people need help to experience your physical self as an endless creative well from which to draw amazing drink, regardless of your age, writing experience, or educational background, you can do this.

Excerpt from The Flying Boy: Healing the Wounded Man

In 1980 I read one of the first articles about Robert Bly's work with men in *New Age Magazine*. While I was moved and completely understood what he was saying, several years passed before I felt the truth told by the man who spoke to me as one who had lived my life. His father was an alcoholic – so was mine. His mother treated him like a magic person and gave him what C.G. Jung terms a "mother complex" – so did mine. He had escaped the world of men – so had I. He said that men who didn't get in touch with their own deep masculinity found themselves unable to make commitments, hold down jobs and have good relationships. They constantly projected their souls onto the women they loved and left. These men did not have male friends because they only trusted females. He called them "Swan Boys" – I was a Flying Boy.

Unconsciously I had denied many things masculine and male in me. Though I looked and dressed like a lumberjack, I kept my hair long like my mother's. I saw maleness as exhibited by my drunken angry father and wanted no part of such meanness. I had seen maleness via the cultural fathers who sent their sons to Vietnam to live out their and John Wayne's dreams of heroism and cultural domination. I wanted nothing to do with such maleness. I looked toward the feminine and tried to look like a sensitive man who would not use his intuition to plough through people's souls and bodies. My spirituality was deeply feminine and finally soft. During my early 30s, thanks to Bly, Laural and others, I realized that I was one who was completely out of balance and quickly approaching a "sickness unto death."

If you fly away from commitments, responsibilities, intimacy, feelings, male friendships and your own body, chances are you are a Flying Boy. If you are a woman reading this, chances are you have loved or come into contact with a Flying Boy.

Flying Boys frequently use fantasy to escape reality. They hide in their mind/intellect and reason to avoid the pain they keep in their bodies. They appear to all but those closest to them as sensitive, gentle, and completely in touch with their feelings. The truth, except in the most extreme circumstances, is that they seldom even know they have bodies and feelings.

Fate and circumstance always seem to be controlling their lives. They can't quite make life work for themselves. When things do begin to work out or they finally succeed at something, they fly off in pursuit of another city, lover, job, degree, religion, or drug.

Flying Boys are often addicted to sex, work, pain, and failure as much as they are to intensity and darkness. They are constantly coming down from ecstatic highs and descending into deep, dramatic depressions. They seek the extremes and are bored with the in-between times.

Flying Boys often grew up in dysfunctional families. Their fathers were both emotionally and physically absent. Their mothers often tried to compensate for this loss. In the process, the Flying Boy learned to reject his masculinity and grew to overvalue the feminine. He experienced his feminine side vicariously through his mother and other mother-like women in his life.

Excerpts from The Flying Boy Letters:
Getting Back to Y'all 30 Years Later

Lower Burrell, PA

Dear John,

I just got done reading your books, **Flying Boy II: The Journey Continues**, and I wanted to write and tell you how much I enjoyed reading it. I related so much to things that you felt and said in your book. I really admired your total honesty.

I had a similar relationship like you had with Lucy to a man who broke it off with me five months ago. I think that an addiction to a person is so much worse than an addiction to a drug. My relationship with this man was like a roller coaster ride all the time. We would get close emotionally, so I thought, only to be dumped than taken back over and over again. Last Fall, when he broke it off with me, this time for good, I tried, like you did with Lucy and Laurel, to make it work. Every time that he would break it off with me, I sometimes felt that he thought that I wasn't good enough for him or something, that he would keep doing this to me.

I know that deep down it is for the best that this happened. I prayed for God's will in this relationship, and I guess God answered my prayers, but not in the way I hoped.

Everything I've heard and everything I've read teaches

you the same thing – you've really got to love yourself. I'm working on this, although I'm still not sure how to go about this. I know you mentioned it in your books about letting go, but how did you get Lucy and Laurel out of your head as well as your heart? How do you really let go?

As you can probably tell, I am looking for answers in my life, and I'm not sure where to find them. I know that I need time to heal and recover and to work on getting my self-esteem back.

I would like to wish you luck for the future in all of your love relationships. Also, keep up the good work of helping people overcome their codependency.

Sincerely,

Roller Coaster Rider

Dear Ms. Roller Coaster Rider:

You're absolutely right! Addiction to a person is much harder for some people to deal with than drugs or alcohol. I know it was for me. We NEED people, love, affection, tenderness, and someone to talk to. We don't NEED drugs or alcohol, but we want and crave them to numb the pain of having needed people in our past like mothers, fathers, mentors, and teachers to show us how to do things like face our fears of intimacy with people we love who don't turn away from us.

So, what do we do if we are in love with the backs of people who keep walking away from us but then make an emotional and physical U-Turn and come back for a little while?

I used to be in love with love and with those beautiful backs. I wanted them back, pursued them to come back, or I'd push them away when intimacy became more than I could handle at the time. Sometimes though – I hate to say it – I would push them away like I did Laurel in The Flying Boy, just to see if I could manipulate them into coming back for another round of our emotional come-here-go away dance.

Occasionally, I was the back that a few women watched walking out the relationship door (including Laurel). I was always hoping, as I headed for the hills, that they would come after me and ask me to come back.

One woman, my former wife, was the only one that came after me after I pushed her away, and I'm so thankful she did. We had about 17 years of togetherness – not perfect – but we at least met each other face to face and I felt really loved and wanted.

Now if you asked me 30 years ago, how did I let go of Laurel – the woman who changed my life and who I wrote about in **The Flying Boy**, and how did I let go of Lucy, the woman in my book, **I Don't Want to Be Alone** (later there was a title change to **Flying Boy Book II: The Journey**

Continues), I'll tell you the truth – now 30 years later – in a way I wouldn't have at the time you wrote your beautiful letter.

I did a radio interview years ago and the host said, "How would you describe the central message of your books and lectures?"

Without a moment's hesitation I answered, "I can sum it up in two words – Let Go."

He quickly responded, "Let go of what?"

To which I replied:

Everything and everyone that you need more than love. Let go of everything we were taught that wasn't right or true, and that's a whole lot. We let go, as adults, of mothers and fathers so we can see and interact with them as flawed people just like we are. We let go of the last stage of life so we can enter the next stage, and then let that one go, and on and on. We let go of searching for happiness outside ourselves, and instead, search for meaning inside ourselves, knowing that it too will have to be let go the more we grow and heal. We let go of all our false selves. All our masks are thrown into the garbage along with all our vanities and needs to be right, important, and famous. We let go of our greed for more and more stuff like houses, cars, and illusions of grandeur, because they are all going to turn to "dust in the wind," as one of my ancient favorite rock groups, Kansas, said dozens of years ago.

You see the more we let go, the more we can enjoy everything we have to a fuller and greater degree. I have several great friends and I try to let them go every day so I can be with them cleaned out and present with them in ways I can't if my goal is to hold on to them. Letting go leads us into a more eternal now than holding on does because holding on constantly forces us to stay in the future or in the past.

Now, going back to your question, which is substantially harder, "How do we let go?" Well, the truth is, I don't know how either even though I've been working on it for thirty-something years since you first wrote. I think of Laurel fairly often, and Lucy and I are friends who still talk to each other and hang out 28 years later.

I still talk about, and teach people, how to let go of the pain they hold in their bodies from the grief and anger they have swallowed, stuffed, and bottled up – sometimes for decades. Yes, I teach about romance, love, and relationship addiction – because we only teach what we need to learn. So honestly, letting go is not my strong suit, but I've gotten better over the years, and I bet you have to by now.

So, I will let you go and send blessings on you for writing.

JOHN

White Bear Lake, Minnesota

Dear John:

I just finished reading **Flying Boy II: The Journey Continues**. As usual, I was so anxious for help that I only read the last half. I'm inspired. It was exactly what I needed. Now, the work begins. I want the end result so bad. I hate codependency. Yesterday when I heard my dad's voice, I felt angry again even though I've forgiven him.

As my lover sleeps and I think of the emotional abuse of each and every day, my heart saddens for my child within me. She's been hurting for 43 years. It's time to care for her now. Your book will help me do that as I re-read and follow through.

I must tell you that as I once again walked directly to the self-help book section at the bookstore your title jumped out at me. I picked it up, read the back cover, then I looked at your picture to surmise whether or not your face "looked" full of wisdom, or at least whether it "looked" like you had more info than I. It was the first time I ever threw the book back on the shelf as fast as I could. All of a sudden, it felt like a tornado inside my head. Why did I react so intensely with that book? This is where guilt took over. I "scarefully" picked it up again. "Hum," I thought, "maybe it's time to face reality."

I'm sure I'm ready, but I'm scared to follow through. I pray that I can learn quickly. I need to heal and I'm over-anxious now that I've read your book.

Thank you for getting me started.

Sincerely,

I'm Over-Anxious Joan

Dear I'm Over-Anxious:

I'm glad you found **I Don't Want to Be Alone (Flying Boy II)**, my second book with Health Communications, Inc. Like many of us who know anxiety all too well, you started in the middle just so you could hurry up and get to the end of the book to see how things turned out for Lucy and me.

You say in your letter that when you heard your dad's voice, you felt angry again even though you've forgiven him.

Well, by now you probably have, but you probably hadn't when you wrote this letter nearly 30 years ago. Let me explain what I mean. As a counselor and unorthodox therapist, I have asked hundreds of clients and workshop participants: "Have you ever forgiven a parent or spouse?" The answer runs something like this: "Oh, thousands of times;" "Many times;" "I have to forgive them every day," and so on.

See, most of us were taught we were supposed to forgive people without walking through the door into the anger room. We were also taught and told nice girls didn't get angry, or that anger was a negative emotion, or that we're not really feeling anger at all—that "anger" is just fear, sadness, and abandonment that has been covered up. So, we become prematurely nice—not authentically nice—because we are holding on to so much anger. I realized that until I felt my feelings of anger, frustration, and disappointment, I couldn't fully forgive anyone.

I would say, and still say to the people I work with, "Why don't you feel your anger, experience it, express it, and get to real forgiveness just once and finally?" Then, once your anger has been appropriately expressed you are able to interact with that person in the present, even a parent or lover, and you are feeling a primary emotion (not a secondary one as most therapists have been taught) and you will not unload the ancient baggage of the past on to someone in the present.

Now here is one more thought about anger before I go to other parts of your letter. Many men and women don't want to let go of their anger at someone because anger is the only fine thread or coarse rope that we use to stay connected. We are afraid if we let go of our anger, we will watch them or us just drift off into space.

The truth is that if we're still using unfelt, unexpressed anger as connecting devices, we're only creating an illusion of connection. Forgiveness, and perhaps love, build a much stronger bridge to people than the frayed rope of anger.

Now, don't get me wrong, there are such egregious abuses that some have experienced that may not ever be forgiven, and that is right in its own way.

Remember this: anger is for getting out of stuck places, i.e., jobs, marriages, families, etc., and grief is for having been in a stuck place for so long.

I love how you said: "…once again I walked directly to the self-help section at the bookstore"—I tried to put up a tent in that section years ago because I wanted to live in the self-help aisle for the rest of my life. "…and your title jumped out at me. I picked it up, read the back cover… It was the first time I ever threw the book back on the shelf as fast as I could… I scarefully picked it up again. 'Hum,' I thought, maybe it's time to face reality."

This reminds me of the time a woman who attended a workshop of mine years ago said she would like to show me a copy of **The Flying Boy**.

When she handed it to me, it was in two halves, torn right through the middle. She said, "This is the copy I gave to my husband five years ago. He immediately looked at and read the back cover and then took it out to his workshop where he took a saw and cut it in half." I understood immediately and then she reached in her bag and pulled out another whole intact copy and said, "This is a copy he bought for himself and wants you to sign it."

Thank you for writing,
JOHN

St. Louis, MO

Dear John:

I need to thank you for your book, **The Flying Boy**. I am in the midst of reading it for the second time. The first reading tore me to pieces and put me back together. I had to become consumed with intense pain before I was willing to take action, which led me to the bookstore at the treatment center I went through for chemical dependency in 1980.

It would look as though my pain's immediate source is being unemployed, broke, and currently trying to let go of a woman who has left me. The pain I am experiencing is the worst I can remember. Your book has shown me that these things are the result of a pain I have always been aware of, running very deep, and anger I thought only the Devil was capable of. You've helped me realize how much work I need. I am deathly afraid of having to go through what you did, hoping I can somehow escape it, or that it won't be necessary.

The first reading, at many passages, brought tears to my eyes. Only recently has my pain been strong enough to allow myself tears, and only this book hitting so close to home has brought them out of me.

The second time reading your book, I stop as certain passages bring back memories as far back as saying my first words and many more painful memories.

I have never felt so completely hopeless and lost as in recent days. All I know is I hate my pain and I want it to stop, and I certainly don't want it to last as long as yours did. In one way, I really don't like knowing how sick I am because it seems like so much to go through. On the other hand, I am grateful and feel like your book saved my life, reaffirming the fact that I have always know that what was in me would kill me before it would go away on its own.

I don't know for sure where to go for the help I know I need. I don't know for sure what kind of help I need; except I know I need a lot. You have many times heard people, when undertaking something say, "If it saves one life, it's worth it." Well, I am writing to verify to you that your book was worth it. If I am ever in Austin, I will look you up and thank you in person. If you are ever coming to St. Louis, I would enjoy meeting you. Please call ahead.

Forever grateful,

Joe L.

Dear Who Never Felt So Hopeless and Lost:

You know what fire and rescue teams try to get into our heads? If you're lost in the wilderness, stay put and they will come find you, and yet nearly everyone tries to find their own way out and they end up getting terribly lost for days or weeks or die out there because they were so afraid no one would come find them.

It's okay to be where you are. Be where you are. Be where you are so that you can move out of it.

Then there's the old saying, when the student is ready, the teacher will come. Once again there is great wisdom in getting still, silent, and trusting that now that you are hopeless and lost someone is on their way.

While we are hating our pain, we must give it time to prepare us for the healing, and God, that's hard to do. I hated my pain so much I did everything I could to numb it with alcohol, women, and work. None of them worked. It was going into the pain, letting myself be scared of where my pain would take me. I felt there was so much in me no firefighter or rescue squad would ever find me if I just stood still and trust and wait, trust, and wait. So, I grew wings and flew from the pain, flying from woman to woman, job to job, beer to beer and rum, whiskey, and vodka. Man, did I rack up some frequent flyer miles on this body. I couldn't commit to anyone or anything too long for fear if I landed someone would find out who I really was and how much wreckage and trauma had been put in my young body as a child and adolescent.

Finally, my soul sickness caught up with me, and like you, I really did have the intellectual awareness at least that, as you said in your letter, "what was in me would kill me before it went away on its own."

So once upon a time, long, long ago in a house on 9th Street in Austin in a shabby house even God wouldn't live in just as the sun was sinking down and the moon was slowly rising, Laurel, the woman who left me saying I was angry and full of sadness came around one more time.

Bottom line, she, the forest ranger of feeling and search party for a young man's pain, came and found me. From dusk until dawn, I was like a newborn colt who fell into the deep grass of her arms and I wept out, screamed out, three decades of pain as she held me and kept saying, while she couldn't come back, she wasn't going away that long night into the darkness that was in me so deep I didn't want her or anyone else to ever see.

So, my friend, like I said years ago when I was playing my own music regularly, "Pain, I love it, it will make me a country singer…" Then there is the whole other point of view, get up off your ass and go find a therapist who has done their own work and who keeps doing it, a counselor who helps take you into your body as well as your brain, a men's group who will support you while, as the poet Rilke says:

"Sometimes a man stands up at supper and walks outdoors and keeps on walking because a church that stands somewhere in the East..."

Translated by Robert Bly

So Dear Never Felt So Helpless, I see you in the woods

while you wait for direction, wait to be found or on the road and looking for that "church" that can help us heal.

JOHN

Norwalk, Connecticut

Dear John:

I just finished your book, **The Flying Boy**, and since I am one, I thought you might be able to provide to me advice regarding a specific issue I've been confronting—and one you've confronted.

First of all, I found your book immensely thought-provoking and enlightening. I share many of the traits you discovered. I'm 41, never married, no male friends, etc., and yet I'm well-liked, professionally successful, and handsome. I've been working in therapy for years on these and other issues with some success but not enough.

Recently I've been focusing on my relationship with my mother, which seems similar to your relationship with yours, but I'm stuck. My therapist is encouraging me to feel and express my anger at my mother. She was very dissatisfied with my father, who was lazy, selfish, distant, etc. My mother enlisted me in her campaign against my father, and I joined wholeheartedly. I saw my mother as victimized, the "good parent," whose life was made miserable by the "bad parent," and so I did whatever I could to compensate for my father's inadequacies. This amounted to never wanting anything, never making any demands on my mother, being as "good" as I possibly could be—in short, doing whatever I could to please her.

The problem is, I now feel as if I'm not entitled to anything. I'm always trying to please the women in my life, and while I generally succeed at that, I don't feel comfortable and satisfied, and so I leave them.

But here's the specific problem I need help with. How do I feel angry at my mother? I can't seem to do it. I bought her act hook, line, and sinker, and whenever I think of her, I feel sad and sorry for her. To feel angry at her seems heartless and ungrateful. After all, she always told me how she sacrificed for me and how hard she worked for me. I understand what I should be angry at her for; I believe I have a right to be angry at her—but I can't seem to feel it. When I try to, I feel bad, and I imagine her mournful face looking so hurt by my anger. She died of cancer when I was 16, and that makes it even harder.

My therapist believes it is crucial that I feel and express my anger at my mother, and I agree. But right now, I simply can't.

Any advice?

Thanks for your book, and I hope things are going well for you.

Sincerely,

I Can't Get Angry at My Mother

Dear I Can't Get Angry at My Mother,

Man, do I get you, and as they say now, "I feel you, Bro." But really, I do. I was able to feel my anger and rage at my father about the time you wrote this letter. I knew he verbally, emotionally, and psychologically abused me. But Mom – she was a saint – or so we all thought back then.

It would be years after **The Flying Boy** came out before I, like you, felt I had to take my mom off the cross and off the pedestal, and even she knew this at the time, saying one day on my then-farm in Asheville: "When are you going to work on me the way you did your father? I know you must have some anger at me."

Man! Was she right! Like you, I saw her as a victim who sacrificed so much to stay with Dad, and I sacrificed so much to be her surrogate husband, counselor, and confidant as we proceeded to alienate Dad, and to a degree, demonized him for his alcoholism and being a poor husband and parent.

When kids replace childhood with adult behaviors as early as you did, and I did, we grow up too fast and stay children and childlike too long. Like you said, you feel "not entitled to anything and you (and so did I) always try to please women," hence the name I gave them, "Flying Boys."

By the way, I got this title from reading and article on Robert Bly, the recognized father of the Men's Movement back in 1981. In it, he told a story probably from Grimm Brothers about a woman who took her boys out in the woods so she could have them all to herself. Eventually the "boys" knew they had to leave their mother and so she turned them into swans. As I read, I knew I was a swan boy, and so I came up with the name "Flying Boy."

So yes, I did my "mother work," but the anger was so buried in me and so deep that my therapist at the time had to use extreme measures—dynamite—to blast me open, using a jackhammer to break me out of denial, and then a chisel and hammer to chip away the residual rage that had been in me for decades of feeling sorry for her and realizing I had a right to finally feel both grief and anger.

You say your therapist is encouraging you to feel and express your pent-up rage at a woman who you loved and lost to cancer when you were 16, but when you try, you "imagine her mournful face looking hurt by my anger." As I'm sure you intellectually know, your mother was a complex person with both good and bad aspects or traits, but you say you simply can't, and you're requesting help. This is what I did, and this is how I'm grateful to say I've helped more than a few men get to this undesirable feeling.

You see, what I came up with is that at 38 to 40 years old I had to work on my Ghost Mother—this is the mother at 19 when she birthed her son (My God, a 19-year-old!). She was still a baby raising a baby, but it is that young, green mother I had to get angry with. It was the twenty- and twenty-five-year-old that turned me into a premature adult. It was this woman that I had to get angry at – not the then-sixty-year-old mother who existed at the time to whom I was expressing my anger. My anger was for the young woman who allowed my father's abuse to occur towards me and who smothered me herself – not for the aging woman living in Florida.

So, what I'm saying is yes, your mother died, but it is the ghost mother that still haunts. It is the Ghost that has to be fully exercised and exorcised out of our bodies and our brains so we can finally grow up, see her as a flawed human, and finally let her go.

Begin by imagining that you are taking the fact that she did the best she could, putting it in a box, and put that box in the closet. I've taught for a long time that all parents pretty much do the best they can with what they have. This sentiment still exists—it's still true, and you still can have those feelings—but putting it aside right now will help you get to work. Then, if you have pictures of your mother when she was young, take those pictures and post them around your rooms and talk to that woman, because that's the woman you're still carrying around with you and the Ghost Mother around whom you need to express your anger. With these two techniques, hopefully your anger will begin to surface. It may be helpful to remind yourself as often as necessary that your mother, who did the best she could, is not being hurt by your expression of appropriate anger. When the anger does come, express it, and keep expressing it until you feel you are done. When you feel done, then you take that box out of the closet, open it up, and now you've got "she did the best she could," but you've also gotten angry at her, and then you put those two together. When you are able to express your anger and combine the woman who faulted you with the understanding of all the ways that she did right by you, you will have a stronger, more complete, and more authentic relationship with this woman who was all too briefly alive during your lifetime.

Another possibility is finding somebody who does psychodrama therapy and having this person pretend to be your mother so you can express the things that you wish to tell your mother. Role playing and dramatization can sometimes bring forth formerly unexpressed emotions. Remember, you are not hurting your mother; you are healing yourself.

Now for the men like me whose old mother is still alive at 86, this woman and I finally found a friendship that is functional and even fun. So, if we let go of our ghosts, feeling everything that has been repressed in our bodies and souls, there is a great possibility of talking and interacting adult-to-adult.

So now you're an aging man like me, and I bet you finally got to your rightful, righteous rage and anger, and I hope you got all the benefits that come with that.

Take care and thank you for writing,

JOHN

Excerpts from Courting a Woman's Soul

"Last night as I was sleeping...
the golden bees
were making white combs
and sweet honey
from my old failures..."

Antonio Machado translated by Robert Bly

By the time I met my friend who became my wife for 16 years, I had failed so many times in my youthful attempts to love and be loved.

Every book I've written in my 35-year career emanates out of my old failures. **Courting a Woman's Soul** is no different.

By the time a man is, say 35, he knows even if he can't say it that the things he has been taught, told, saw, and heard from his peers, Playboys, and yes, even his parents, do not work in life or love.

Like most "straight" young men, I was only seeing, no – worshipping, the bodies of the women I slept with or wanted to sleep with. I was un-tutored and un-emotionally intelligent.

By my 40s, thanks to about a million hours of therapy, recovery, and men's work, I finally was yearning to see something eternal – for a glimpse of a woman's soul, bare of society's makeup and my upbringing. I wanted to see the beauty that time and knowing enhances. Now don't get me wrong – I can still enter the slip stream of my own latent narcissism and regress back to adolescence from time to time.

Here are just a few lines from **Courting a Woman's Soul** about the moment I stopped being a naïve, irresponsible boy:

We are not going to be lovers, are we, Isabella asked timidly.

No, Isabella. You deserve the kind of love I can't give

you... If we made love, I would be one more pathetic jerk included on the list of men who have hurt you. I have hurt enough women in my life.

Why had it taken me nearly four decades to realize the difference between lust and love?

Lust takes everything and gives nothing; love gives everything and takes so little.

At first when I was working on "**Courting**" I didn't have a title. I asked my wife (my ex-wife and still best friend) why she picked me to love and marry. Without a moment's hesitation she said, "That easy. You're the only man who ever courted my soul."

> *"...Now you are no longer caught*
> *in the obsession with darkness,*
> *and a desire for higher love-making*
> *sweeps you upward."*

Johann Wolfgang von Goethe

In Search of the Feminine

"It still hasn't occurred to Western man
to stop looking on woman

as a symbol of something and
to begin seeing her simply as woman –
as a human being."

Robert Johnson

Still here in 2020, most men are unconsciously searching for their own feminine part of their being in the faces, eyes, and bodies of women.

Ironically, the patriarchal mentality which still rules is what drove the Feminine almost completely out of culture and a man's individual life.

When men finally start removing our projections of the Feminine from women, we can develop the strengths of our own Feminine or what C.G. Jung called our "anima." When this is in process, it completes and compliments our own masculinity in a healthy positive way.

This connection not only makes a man more human, it allows him to see women – from mother, to lover, to sister, and female friend – as human beings and not as a repository for his own Feminine part of his soul and psyche.

If this is not accomplished, or I should say in the on-going process of being accomplished, by mid-life or older, the man who hasn't accessed his interior Feminine may become ill, seized by a depression, lose interest in life, or find himself angry and abusive towards women in general.

If a woman should feel and/or say to her women friends, "I wish my husband would court my soul," she may mean a number of things but some of the things she actually means is that she wants her husband, lover, or partner to be more attentive, thoughtful, and show her more feeling.

A man who is stunted in his ability to feel and express emotions will not see, cherish, and hold dear a woman's soul.

Without a man's ability to reclaim his own Feminine he will believe unconsciously what way too many men believe that it is a woman's responsibility to make his life whole, keep him happy, give his life meaning, and intensity and ecstasy. This is not a woman's job.

If a man finds his Feminine, he finds his soul, and he will see a woman's soul instead of only her physical appearance and court that woman's soul now and possibly forever.

**Courting the Souls of the Ones You Love:
The Platinum Rule of Loving**

I was forty-something and still longing to be loved the way I needed to be. She had the same longing. Misguided like a missile missing its target, I practiced the "Golden

Rule" – "Do unto others as you would have them do unto you." So, I tried to send her love the way I wanted to be shown – showing up with flowers, buying odd little gifts from Australia or New Zealand where I spoke for years.

She would sigh and set the flowers in a vase in the curio or on the mantle, and I couldn't understand where her enthusiasm for such gifts had gone.

Then one day, quite by accident, with no conscious thought to it, I took the rough draft of my third book into her office and said, "I'd like for you to read this and tell me what you think."

She burst into tears and sobbed for several minutes. I'm good with tears but I wanted to understand what the hell was going on. Slowly she stopped crying.

"Would you tell me why this touched you so deeply?" I asked.

"This is the first time you have asked me to read your work. You usually send it to Robert or Bill first. Thank you so much for loving me so respectfully."

"Damn!" I said, "I didn't know you really would enjoy the books about men. I highly respect your intelligence and would always value your input on my work."

The next day I came home from work and found she had bought me several little gifts that touched me so deeply I broke down and sobbed.

You see I stumbled on to the "Platinum Rule of Love" –
Do unto others the way they have been longing for probably
their whole lives. In other words, send the people you love
– partners, parents, children, husbands, and wives – the way
they, not you, the way they can feel loved. If you don't know
how they want to be loved, here's an idea, ask them.

Last night you looked at me
So lovingly I had to turn away.
A friend said to me
There are two ways to love
Face-to-face, eye-to-eye,
Skin-to-skin
And in the other way
We give love at a distance
And hope they pick up the clues
Yesterday I brought you a
Dozen red roses and each
One was a clue and a promise
Someday I would learn to
Love the open way of the flower.

Excerpt Where Do I Go from Her?

Search and Rescue workers have been trying to tell people for years that when you are lost in the woods just stay where you are, and they will come and find you. The main reason folks end up in critical situations is because they are afraid to stay where they are and that no one will find them. So off they go, searching for a way out, and they can't be found until days, weeks—or never. I'm going to stay here and wait and write my feelings, thoughts, and reflections until someone finds me. I'm going to try and figure out where do I go from her.

When we were gullible kids my friends and I actually thought if we dug hard enough, long enough, and deep enough we'd come out in China. So, we kept digging. When we were teenagers, we thought if we wanted to be rock stars badly enough, it didn't really matter that no one knew how to play an instrument; we just formed a band. When we went to college, we actually thought we could marry the captain of the team or the head majorette if they could just get past the fact that we weren't as beautiful as they. When we got married, we actually thought we could stay in love forever— but as it turned out digging a hole in the backyard was really more doable than the subsequent separating, divorce, or death, and then the surviving and moving forward.

I'm writing most of this most unusual memoir at my

mountain home in the foothills of the Appalachians. Sometimes I even talk to this mountain, along the lines of, "So what do I do now?" I also sometimes hear a response: "Be silent and wait like I have for thousands and thousands of years." Dog lovers will not think I'm totally nuts as I speak to my Giant Alaskan Malamute who lays loyally by my feet. "And you? Anything to contribute to this process of letting go?" She always replies the same thing, "Learn to pull something ten times your own weight and then we'll really talk." One night, as I stared at the chessboard my former wife gave me one Christmas, and I swear it said, "Sometimes the king is the first to go." Novels I've read, formerly sitting quietly on several dozen bookshelves, whispered, "Love has no clean-cut beginning, middle, or end." I told them all their advice was solid, picked up my favorite poet's book, and randomly opened it to the page that read, "Once you have loved someone you will always love them." And to that all I can do is say, "Amen."

"I love what I do not have. You are so far…"

Pablo Neruda

It seems to be a fact that loving is so short and forgetting is so God-damn long. That's all I need to say most days, but I'll scribble some more words into this leather-bound journal that no one may read. Hell, like most of my journals it will probably sit passively on shelves receiving dust. So why take the time? Like my journal teacher in abstention, the dearly departed May Sarton says, "Why talk about it? I say, talk about it because these are the things we bury and never do bring out into the open. And what is a journal for if they are never mentioned?"

When X first told me about her need to divorce, I left my body, hovering, clinging to the ceiling, certain I'd come back down. Now days have passed, and months have passed and even years have passed. I try to reinhabit my body and make my soul catch up with the fact that while we send pictures of our cats and dogs to each other through email, there are few words between us—a text here and there—and sadness becomes sorrow.

Yesterday my young friend Kat asked, "What is the difference between sadness and sorrow?" I've never been asked that question, nor have I felt the need to distinguish the two. But I think of sadness as an emotion that comes naturally if one allows, and it goes and then it comes again as life dictates. Right now, it would seem I am in a permanent state of sorrow, a feeling that will be less, greater, even greater, and less again but at this moment feels like a river that will never make it to the sea.

Sadness is as transient as joy, lasts as long as laughter or fear, and then disappears altogether with the new arrival of things—good news, a promotion, a book deal, a new love.

But sorrow is four seasons long, it is the constant backdrop for the play that continues though the setting, character, and time changes.

Sadness is, "she's gone," and sorrow is, "she's not coming back." This is reinforced everywhere you look, felt every time you see the candleholder you bought together or the painting you picked out to hang in the living room of your cottage, felt every time any song from Bach to Beatles is played no matter how different the setting. Sadness is seeing doors shut. Sorrow is seeing them sealed. But sadness and sorrow can also become the creators of a new life, a new vision, a revived energy, enthusiasm, and guide. But first I had to learn to navigate the uncharted territories of divorce, disease, depression, despair and get to a land where love grows out of the ground of a new kind of a sacred, secular faith. This is not the kind of faith of our fathers and mothers and forefathers and mothers, not written in holy books, taught and told by priests, preachers, gurus, and Rabbis but more likely referenced by poets such as David Whyte who wrote "…When your vision is gone no part of the world can find you…Give up all the other worlds except the one to which you belong…" This is where I know Faith—or at least this man's faith—may be found.

I went to my cottage in the pigmy mountains of North Alabama and started unbecoming all I'd been in order to become who I am meant to be. This journey while still being taken started with a journal. This is what happened, and this is what I felt and learned when my vision, my wife, and my life disappeared.

Excerpts from A Quiet Strength: Meditations on the Masculine Soul

"A thoughtful book like this encourages contemplation, rather than hyperactivity, and, oddly, we need good words in order to find fruitful silence."

Thomas Moore, *Care of the Soul*

Who will mentor, teach, and touch the souls of the boys who have been bullied, bloodied, and beaten literally or figuratively?

Making Peace

"Blessed are the peacemakers." Matthew 5:9

Many men are uncomfortable with peace though we may

like the idea. We've been programmed since childhood to prepare for war, prepare to kill or be killed. We played army at five years old, imagining sticks into sub-machine guns, dirt clods into grenades, pretending to sneak up on the enemy to destroy them. Later on, some of us went on to wage wars on battlefields known as gridirons. If we didn't engage in combat there, then we did with fellow classmates particularly the ones who tried to wrestle away our girlfriends. We carried our propensity for battle into bedrooms and corporate boardrooms believing our manhood would be won or lost there.

Without a war to fight we rested only to prepare for the next great conflict, the next chance to "prove our strength." We came to associate peace with boredom.

I want to teach my children that peace is greater than pistols, quiet and contentment more necessary than counterattack.

Today I'll make peace with an old friend or relative I've hurt, a child I wounded with words. If nothing else, I'll declare a cease-fire with myself. I'll refuse to shame myself for learning what I was taught.

Returning the Earth

"We have conquered the environment, and in our obsession for control, we no longer allow the environment to live in us."

Valerie Andrews

Humankind has "tamed" the wilderness, bought, and sold land for profit and loss. For too long we have mortgaged the earth and bankrupted its resources, pouring fumes into the skies and sludge into the oceans as if they were ours to destroy. Much more than rhetoric and legislation are needed to change this pattern of control and conquest over nature. I must begin a new inner relationship to my environment. Only then will the right action be clear to me.

I resolve to let the great trees live in me. I accept their strength and the wisdom of their years. I invite the land back into my legs and back and bones so that I might reclaim the rhythms of birth, death, and renewal. As I stand on the shore, I'll feel the sea rushing into my gut. I'll let my arms reach to embrace the painted sky. I'll walk right through the mud! I'll receive the meaning of those mountains at which I used to blankly stare wondering who "owned" them. To be truly alive, I must relinquish my illusions. To truly survive, I must learn to receive the grace of this earth with gratitude, respect, and love.

Today I let go of the illusion of control, the dogma of dominion. I set my soul on automatic pilot, letting it soar through this world. Today I am touched and taught by the earth.

Earth, the Great Teacher

"Speak to the earth, and it shall teach thee." Job 12:8

So many men have been brainwashed into believing that the Earth is not alive, that it possesses no character, no feeling, and that it's merely here to serve the insatiable demands of a greedy few. As we recover from this soul-shattering falsehood a new depth of experience enters our life: we hear the Earth speak, groan, sign, and yes, bless us for listening to her cries.

The deeper I delve into the truth of my own body and soul the deeper the teachings I receive from the Earth. That teaching is never stale, never inappropriate – each one of us will learn something different from the Earth, the first and last Mother and Father to us all.

Today I'll listen to the truth the Earth has to teach.

A Wordless Language

"Nature is one of the languages God speaks."

Robert Bly

Many men have dabbled in, even mastered, languages. We speak fluent English, manage German "ein bischen," use a peso's worth of Spanish, murmur French when we feel amorous. We understand well the language of commerce, of industry. We're plainspoken about stocks and bonds. We know "car talk." We're conversant in the colorful idioms of sports.

Every language has its proper place and time. And language is fun, even grandly mysterious at times. But for us to know and feel that point at which we and our God become one, we must speak the language of nature from time to time. We listen to God's messages there, in the mountains, forests, lakes, and sky. The message is usually brief, and it's delivered easily, right into the body and soul.

Today I'll receive the wind's whispers, the speech of the stream, the valley's still, small voice. If I can be still amidst change as they are, I will become fluent in field, stone, tree, and fire.

The Language of Animals

"Animals are nothing but the forms of our virtues and

vices, wandering before our eyes, the visible phantoms of our souls."

Victor Hugo

Men used to listen attentively to the messages of the animals; our lives, our souls, depended on it. The appearances and absences of certain animals at certain times were full of meaning and offered essential guidance. The hawk, raven, wolf, and bear all sent messages to men and spoke in a language we understood.

A part of us still understands that language. The animals still speak, showing up at interesting times, in "coincidental" ways. A husky, a cousin to the wolf, might walk up to us just when we are in need of courage. A cat visits when we require patience. When peace is most precious, a dove flies overhead. The animals are speaking.

Today I'll observe the animals to absorb their wisdom.

The True Work

"Blessed is who has found his work; let him ask no other blessedness."

Thomas Carlyle

The work we do should feed our soul and keep it strong as good food nourishes the body. Sometimes we work only for money and survival because it may be that that's all we can do at the moment. But often we work this way because we're living someone else's life rather than our own. Are we working to bring a father's, or a mother's, dreams to fruition? Or perhaps we have convinced ourselves that it's better to be rich than happy. Do we believe the two are mutually exclusive? We must reflect on these questions with courage to find out whether we're doing work that blesses ourselves and others.

Before the years run out, we need to be sure we're not running from our heart's desire out of fear or a desire for approval. We must be true to our inner life because it's the only life we can be certain of.

Today I'll look at my work. If it doesn't ring true, if it's not "my bliss," I'll do some interior work necessary to discover my next step. If I find that I'm doing what I'm meant to do, then it falls to me to feel thankful.

Deep Respect

"Our capacity for intimacy is built on deep respect, a presence that allows what is true to express itself, to be discovered."

Jack Kornfield

Respect can connect humans at the deepest level. Love that is based on respect – rather than need or longing – is more enduring. Such respect can tolerate great differences. Truth and commitment can emerge in the container of mutual respect.

Some things command our respect – perhaps because of their beauty or power. Respect for the ordinary, especially in intimate relationships, can sustain those connections. Express your respect. Say it. Show it in a gift or gesture, especially during difficult times. That which is accompanied with respect, even if it is difficult, will be better heard.

Today I will respect myself and all others whom I have contact with. I will communicate that respect by what I do and say.

Fire

"The voice at the center speaks in tongues of flame ... The child in man hears his fire rise."

M. C. Richards

The author of the quotation above, M. C. Richards, is a potter. Fire is at the center of her art, as it is at the center of much art – indeed, of life itself. The blaze captures our gaze. Love, like fire, can sear, is not always kind, can cut through the dead wood, demanding change. Solar fire lights each day; without it we would perish instantly. The sun rises brilliantly some mornings, giving us pleasure and another new day. The sources of fire are many: relationships, the sun, a forest burning wildly, and wherever friction exits. Fire is many things:

strength, power, destruction, beauty.

Some people so fear fire that they never allow its flames to ignite them. They become passive, missing the activity inherent in fire. Others move too often into the fire and are frequently burned. Crafting the appropriate relationship to fire and to fiery people is key.

Today I will reflect on fire. I may light a fire in a fireplace, or make a fire on a beach, in my backyard, or elsewhere. As I watch the flames leap, I will think about how to kindle the fire in my heart.

Youth

"In the woods is perpetual youth."

Ralph Waldo Emerson

Because our society is so youth-oriented, many men want to "stay young." Compounding the problem is the fact that so many of us as boys were made to grow up too fast. It's as though we lost our youth before we ever had it – becoming too responsible and too serious before our time. Yet many fifty- and sixty-year-old men still feel and act like boys regarding relationships, commitment, and direction in life. These men have a lot of Puer (Eternal Youth) in them. This is the "boy in the man's body" syndrome, the Flying Boy.

Of course, there is a big difference between "perpetual"

youth and "eternal" youth. The man who knows nature, who loves the ancient places, who often roams the woods and meadows stays perpetually young inside. This doesn't mean he stops making decisions and commitments. Instead, he stays clear about his responsibilities because of the rejuvenating freedom he feels as he moves through the wide world.

Today I'll honor the Flying Boy, the Puer. In this way, I can hold a fresh, youthful outlook, part of which is not caring whether or not I look young.

Where is the Treasure?

"If there is to be any peace it will come through being, not having."

Henry Miller

As boys, many of us learned that having a lot of toys brought popularity. As teenagers, whoever had the first car was the center of attention. If we had more clothes, money, and athletic ability, we had more dates and others envied us. To this day, many of us still seek happiness in things – a better car, a gold credit card, a more spacious house – more, always more. Where is our satisfaction? Aren't the things we have now the things we wanted a few years ago and worked so hard to achieve? Where is the contentment, the enjoyment we expected to feel?

There's nothing wrong with possessions of course. It's great to feel gratitude for what we've received in our lives. But if we feel driven to get more, to accomplish more and more, maybe our desire is misplaced. What we really want most is not to be found outside us. Throughout the ages, the wise ones have said that the love we give and receive in this life is all we take with us when it's over. Together we can focus on acquiring inner peace. Then by our example, we will leave our sons and daughters this great treasure, a wealth they can never lose.

Today I'll look at how much time I spend getting, how much I spend giving, and how much I spend just being. I have the power to change the focus of my time and life to reflect the highest good.

Conflict

"In fact, the conflict itself is creative and perhaps should never be healed."

Thomas Moore

Very often men seek to remove conflict. At times that's the best move to make. But hoping for an end to all conflict is un-realistic. Conflict is natural; it's part of living in community rather than isolation.

When conflict arises, I can take it as a great opportunity to practice my skills. I can explore, appreciate, and learn from each circumstance. If someone flirts with my wife, I get to practice handling my jealousy and anger. In a disagreement with a coworker, I can practice seeking a task in a new way. If my teenage son wants to dye his hair purple and put a ring in his nose, I get to practice tolerance and compromise.

No matter how disagreeable on the outside, every conflict has a delicious sweet at its core – a great teaching hidden in its middle. To pray that a conflict will disappear before it has done its work on me will only lead me further into darkness. To meet conflicts with an enthusiastic good nature, to work at each one until I discover its hidden teaching, is to live wisely and fully.

Today I accept the presence of conflict in my life. I have the choice to embrace conflicts, to learn from them, to use them to grow.

PART 3

PERSONAL STORIES

Life Is A Funny Old Dog

In Alabama, if you meet someone you know you say, "How's your momma'n'em?" If you don't know them, you say hello, pass some pleasantries, and then you say, "So who are your people?" Let me answer this question.

These are my people, at least the people on the Knight and Lee sides of the family. I came from grandparents who were sharecroppers for a long time before they owned their own small farms. They plowed with borrowed mules before they bought their own tractors. Both my grandfathers and their fathers slaughtered hogs at the hint of the first frost and ate everything that surly pig begrudgingly gave up. My great-grandmothers called their husbands Mister, and Mister washed his feet in a pan every Saturday night, and sometimes he washed the feet of his brethren on Sunday mornings, being the Baptist he was brought up to be.

The water they used to wash their sins away came from creeks, ponds, and wells instead of water faucets. Cooking water was drawn from ice-cold wells by hands as rough as corn cobs. The wells were found by water witchers using forked branches from an old oak tree.

My people were old when they were in their 40s, and grandparents were old way before then, since many of them were bound together for life at 13 or 14. Being 19 for a woman was considered really bad news because she was labeled an old maid or spinster.

My people hunted and ate squirrels, rabbits, and possums, saying grace and thanking the Lord for them. They blew rabbit tobacco or cigar smoke in their children's ears when they suffered from an earache, and if grandpa's nose itched that meant someone was coming, and if their ears burned that meant someone was talking about them. They didn't believe in doctors, and even if they did, they didn't have the money to pay for one, so they relied on a lot of old ways. If their kids had a sty they would chant, "Sty, sty leave his eye, catch the next one who walks by." If frogs gave you warts, witchery could remove them, and no one thought the Holy Ghost would mind a little witchery every now and then. Most of them tended, except tee-totalers, to make, distribute and worship White Lightnin' since it weren't no sin if used for medicinal purposes or to get their rear in gear for a Saturday night fight or for square dancin'.

Most of them were uneducated and didn't trust anyone who was, and yet would walk two inches taller when their children learned to read "real good." But they knew when to sow and when to reap, and how deep to plant a seed, and had the patience to watch it, and watch their children, grow – though childhood was short and usually over by age eight or nine. While they weren't great readers themselves, they were damn good story tellers and nearly everyone was musical in some way and ready to pick and grin the night away, belting out a Jimmy Rogers' or Hank Williams' song without much shyness. Many a grandma beat the black off the keys of an upright, slightly out of tune pianne' and belt out "The Old Rugged Cross" fully believing she would exchange that cross "someday for a crown."

I came from men who wouldn't hold a baby for fear they might break it and who wouldn't hold hands with their four-year-old or their wife in public because that was too personal. But they thought it was their duty to toughen up and break boys before they were the ripe old age of eight or nine—for the most part, girls didn't get "broken" until 12 or 13.

I came from men who hand-rolled their Prince Albert cigarettes, and later smoked two or three packs of unfiltered cancer sticks a day and drank lots of Old Crow whiskey at night and especially on weekends after working in northern factories, which was supposed to provide a better living than a few acres of worn-out soil down South. These men thought a handshake was as good as a signature on a piece of paper. These men were rough on their children and their women, but even worse on themselves, especially if they were unemployed or underemployed.

I came from women who not only stood by their men but would help them stand up in court or in church after a hard night. They had to hide money to buy shoes and picked cotton as good as any man alive. These women doted on their children since the fathers were either gone in the fields, and later to the factories, trying to compensate for their husband's coldness and indifference and pure lack of what we now call "emotional intelligence." I came from women who read the Bible, made their own clothes, and thought a Sears and Roebuck catalogue was about as close as they would ever come to being middle class.

Where did most of these people come from? They sailed across the big pond from Scotland and Ireland. Most of them settled in Alabama, Georgia, Tennessee, Virginia, the Carolinas, and a few went to, "M-I-crooked-letter-crooked letter-I-crooked-letter-crooked-letter-I-humpback-humpback-I": That's how we learned to spell Mississippi. Most of the land had petered out due to over-farming and not rotating the crops, and a lot of what was left was strangled by kudzu, and yet these are some of the most beautiful states in the Union and some of the greatest and most religious and spiritual people in the world.

It was here in the Deep South that I found myself still struggling with leftover Puritanism. My people would be working for the people who John Winthrop said would be owning the "shining city upon a hill." This exclusive Christian club worked for me for a while, but then it got to be like the vegetable your mom or dad puts on your plate saying, "Eat this; it is good for you," but you don't really like the taste, so you hide it under the mashed potatoes and hope they don't notice. Fundamentalist Christianity became my own personal Brussels sprouts and psychology my lumpy mashed potatoes. I was hiding my doubts about the little baby Jesus who was supposedly born in a manger to a virgin as well as the one who bled on the cross for my sins. Mixed into the mess was a whole plate full of self-dished-out shame and guilt that I couldn't do what I thought and was even told I was born to do—be a preacher.

So, I became a professor of Religious Studies at the university and a teacher. Mom had to settle for second best.

Machine Shop

I worked in my dad's machine shop after school and on Saturdays and sometimes on Sundays. During the summer he would give me a full week's vacation with pay and I'd go and visit my granddaddy and grandma on his side of the family.

It was there that I found a little comfort and caring when I wasn't cleaning out one or two of his four chicken houses or getting my hands pecked by mamas who didn't want to give up their eggs. Even there I'd have to earn my keep by cleaning out their nests after they had laid all the eggs they could and been shipped off to Colonel Sanders. It was as brutal job as any nine-to-twelve-year-old boy ever had.

The only enjoyable thing about it was getting to be with my granddaddy, a small man named Audie, and my grandmother, Addie. Both were so diminutive I'll never know how they produced a six-foot, two-inch son.

Granddad let me do three things. After the chickens were cleared out, he would let me and my red-haired, freckle-faced cousin Donald, go shoot rats with our 22's. We'd become excellent marksman in our minds having killed everything from empty Coke bottles to crows. We'd compete to see which of us was the best rat murderer, sitting for hours in silence waiting for one to make a run for it. Pop! Pop! Pop! Three for him, none for me, most nights. My sights must have been off or tampered with by my villainous red-haired, citified cousin.

The other thing my granddad and I did was watch The Lester Flat and Earl Scruggs Show, and Porter Wagoner shows on Saturday nights while he washed his feet in a pan of hot water, brought to him by his dutiful wife, who sometimes referred to him as mister. After hearing the best banjo picking in the world, Saturday night wrestling—the most unnatural and unauthentic sport that has ever been—he would pull down a jar of peppermint sticks. We'd suck on one or two as the guys threw their opponents over the ropes and picked up folding chairs to seriously bash over their backs. Were we in redneck nirvana or what?

I couldn't wait to get back on my grandfather's safe island from the sea of chaos at home, but like all good things end, he died too young and too soon. Audie Lee died at the same age I am right now as I write this tiny eulogy.

This was a man my father did not know. I got the common sense and compassion that old age and experience had brought to my grandfather. The Dr. Peppers and Cokes Granddaddy bought for me when we went to Crossville became paper cuts to my dad's soul.

Pagans, Poetry, and Passions

The University of North Alabama, formerly Florence State College, formerly Florence State Teacher's College, spread out before me waiting to suck me into its academic belly, digest me and spit me out an educated hillbilly, redneck, salesman, boozer, and babe chaser, and send me on to seminary and then out into the wicked world to preach the gospel according to me. What a system! If I could crack it anybody can.

Those first few months I learned a lot—mainly that goofing off with my best buds, Bob White, Roger Fuller and Dane Dixon, all through high school and irritating teachers to get a laugh had left me virtually illiterate. So, I began reading not only what was expected in each course, but everything I could every waking hour. I carried paperbacks in the back pockets of my Levi's and would pull them out even in the bathroom—every moment was precious, and I didn't want to waste any of them. I had a lot of catching up to do. Although I was sucking hind tit compared to my compatriots in class, it didn't dissuade me from thinking I was chosen by God almighty to spread the word of Jesus Christ to the rest of the heathens around me.

Somehow, I got signed up with the local Methodist ministries to become a substitute minister.

When the regular pastor could not be present to preach and attend to his flock, they would give neophytes like me, who were preparing for the ministry a call, and we'd mount our white horses, or in my case, a rusty, blue Chevy Vega, and go pretend we knew what the hell we were talking about at the tender age of twenty-one or -two. I thought surely this would impress my red-haired angel Phyllis that I really wanted much more than Jesus.

Somewhere along my way to getting on "The Dean's List," I started veering off the straight and narrow. Something was pulling me. Was it Satan, the great seducer of potential seminary students? Beelzebub, the Devil himself trying to penetrate my psyche (Greek word meaning soul) – see Dean, how much I learned? Was I such a treat to Lucifer's diabolical plan, the old serpent himself that sent me towards the pagan professors, back-sliding preachers and weirdo poets who became a huge influence on me in ways I didn't even know at the time?

I had taken a few sociology classes before I was asked to leave college back in 1970. I had to declare a major upon returning. I had done pretty well according to my transcripts—two D's and one C—Sociology it was. Besides even would-be saints like myself needed to know about the society I'd be preaching in and to, and there was nothing that went against the Gospels. But then there was the electives and courses that would transfer into most any seminaries that would take me – courses like The New Testament and The Old Testament. Every upstart Bible-banger needed those, but here is where the slippery slope that led right to Hell began— The History of World Religion, Comparative Religion – they were teaching the heretical ideas that there were religions besides Christianity that had satisfied and soothed souls for centuries and some even before Christ came to earth.

Dr. Miller (I'll call him) was a short, cheery, Episcopal priest in his late 70s or early 80s that taught these pagan philosophies. Turns out the word "pagan" comes from the Greek or Latin word, I forget which, "Pagano's," which means "country folk." I could relate. I took every course this distinguished, easy-going, gray-haired man taught as my back began to accumulate marks from the slide, I was taking by giving credence to these blasphemous creeds. So, while I'm studying the historical veracity, or lack of the Four Gospels, I'm also being introduced to Lao Tzu, Confucius, Buddha, Shintoism and much more all the while eating it up with a spoon.

Now to make matters worse I was accumulating quality points, becoming Vice-President of the Sociology Club, and meeting non-believers who had to be the Devil's henchmen because a couple of them, Ed, and Dan, introduced me to the poetry teacher they admired. Dan and Ed were two aspiring poets themselves. We would meet in the Student Union for coffee and conversation, not conversion, well maybe they were converting me. Dan reminded me of a southern version of James Dean—tall, lanky, tanned, and intelligent. His cohort Ed was shorter, studious-looking, and eccentric.

"You've got to take a course from Dr. Thompson," was their almost daily battle cry.

"I don't know guys; English is not my forte. I mean I've barely mastered Southern Appalachian and I'm almost finished with my hours to complete my bachelor's in sociology."

"Listen, Dr. John Thompson will blow your fucking mind. Sorry, I forgot you don't curse," said Dan jokingly. I was trying to stay with my self-imposed asceticism—no cursing, screwing, drinking, smoking or caffeine.

My mind had already suffered a serious shock by exposure to Eastern thought. I wasn't sure my neocortex was developed enough to handle more disruption.

After many more hours of brow beating, I gave up and went to registration for the next semester and signed up for Dr. Thompson's Advanced Romantic Poetry class.

Let the Inquisition of my faith begin.

School-Dazed and Confused

"A 0.02 average," the white-haired Dean of Students said with a mixture of sarcasm and disbelief in his voice. He took off his glasses, pinched his nose and rubbed it before looking up from my transcripts. The bookish man with girlish fingers laid his wire-rimmed glasses on the table and looked around the four tables in a square that had been placed in the cavernous cafeteria as a makeshift courtroom that would decide mine and others' fates who had murdered their chances at a college education.

I sat there at the opposite end of their world, a stranger in a strange land, knowing I didn't speak their language.

"Can you tell us here why we should agree to let you back in with a record like this?" he said looking at the others but not directly at me.

"Yes sir," was all I could think of to say at the moment.

"Tell this esteemed body why you want to come back to college. But before you begin, I want to say two things. I think I can speak for everyone at this table. First, I don't think I can ever recall someone with your record asking to be admitted a second time, and second, I can't believe you can say anything that would convince us of your seriousness and gravitas to seek a genuine education. Now it is your turn, Mr.

Lee. We are all ears."

I was lucky I knew what the word serious meant, but I had no idea what the hell gravitas meant. I sat there thinking that before my Christian days I would have thought what an ass-hole, but I was bucking for sainthood then and had given up cursing a year before to impress that red-haired Christian girl.

"I want to be a preacher and a teacher. I believe with all my heart that is what I've been put on this earth to do, sir."

Everyone, especially the Dean, looked like I was talking like a tree had fallen on me, as we say in the South, which for you northerners, means talking like I was crazy. The silence was deafening as the corduroy-elbow-patched professors and the two women who wore their hair in a tight bun broke in to syncopated laughter.

"Mr. Lee, I have to hand it to you. That is the most original answer I think we've ever heard at one of these and I think I can speak for everyone here. What a thought—a 0.02 student aspires to be a teacher and a preacher. Well good luck, son. I know you are going to need God's help because you have got one hell of a job in front of you. I think," he paused to collect himself and wait for everyone to stop laughing, "We all agree to let you in for a probationary period of two semesters. If you show yourself to be a serious scholar in the making, then you can stay. You really want to be a preacher and a teacher?

That's just the most outrageous and original answer I've ever heard."

I was in to learn this time and couldn't wait to see what would come next.

PART 4

POETRY

Some Marriages

Some marriages are great
symmetrical structures made from
a deck of playing cards. Everything
stacks up so well.

Then a strong, cruel, October
wind blows those lined up
cardboards and they become
birds that soar everywhere.

The ace of clubs flies up
into someone's sleeve, perhaps
up the arm of someone
we've never met before.

The wild deuces head
for the West Texas desert,
while the King and Queen sleep
in separate beds.

The lazy black jack buys
a house in the suburbs
and pays for the ten of hearts
to go back to college.

The rest of the deck quotes
Rilke as they all ascend
into the heavens whispering,
"Let everything happen to you: beauty and terror."

Noisy Silence

There is a kind of noisy silence
some marriages make. Husbands
become devoted to it, and it makes
vows squeak like a rusty
front porch swing. A woman
lies next to a quiet man
for twenty or thirty years
alone in the dark. His breathing
turns her body into stone. She
seldom sleeps. She stares
at the ceiling and remembers how
she married young and "for love."
Now she just waits for morning.

Thunderstorm In Mentone

The wind is different tonight.
The leaves on the trees move easily.

Summer rain cleans the horses
grazing in the wet grass in the pasture
across the road.

I saw lightning for the first time
in months. It looked like a ragged
tuning fork, and I felt the thunder
roll through my body.

Today, in a house a hundred miles
away I saw my father for the first
time in ten years.

He sat beside me with his bare shoulder
against mine as we looked at a map.
Years ago, I would have wanted more to
happen and felt a disappointment,
but this meeting moved easily.
A part of me (the part that always wanted more)
felt cleaned. The lightning comes
down in straight lines and then
separates into its tines. A father and son
and a tuning fork are like that too.

We talked about gas mileage; then
he showed me the peas he's grown in his garden.
This is the most affection I am going
To get, I thought.

Today this amount of affection was finally enough.

Holding On

There is always one leaf
that hangs on to certain trees
even in mid-January – wind
blowing thirty miles an hour.

It holds on the way a bowl holds on
to a Buddhist monk, a Bible holds
on to a Christian; the way a cane
holds on to a blind man.

What holds on to me when it's winter?
A poker perhaps to poke and stir the
fire, a pen that turns empty white
paper into a prayer for some company.

Every morning I sit down by
the fire. I see the poker by my hand,
the pen on the table and, outside, the
leaf still holding on.

Ancient Paths

Geese know the ancient path
their parents laid out for them
in the sky.
When horses are born
the first thing they do is walk,
even if their legs are like water.
Animals seem to know what to do
when it's time.

I remember the first time
a woman said, "Let me hold you."
This was a path I could not remember.
I turned and twisted my body like a
colt leaving the birth canal.
Finally, I fell into the deep grass of her arms.
I lay on my left arm
till it went sound asleep.
Unlike the newborn, I didn't care if I ever
stood on my own two feet
again.

The Long Walk Home

I drive up the mountain.
I'm too modern to walk.
Once on top I watch the
cattle graze, and men in gimme
caps plowing their fields
I notice the wild Tiger
Lilies how they connect
one neighbor's farm to the next.

If we still walked up mountains
would I know how to pray?
I park my car and find a picnic
table that overlooks the valley.
As I do, a black ant crawls
toward my white page.
I take a deep breath – and blow it
eighteen or twenty inches away –
and then just as determined as before,
it proceeds to come back towards me.

John Lee

John Lee has been a professional teacher, author, counselor, and life coach for 30 years. He began as a graduate teaching assistant at The University of Alabama and upon completing his master's degree he was hired as an Instructor in the English and American Studies departments for two years. Lee left Alabama to pursue his doctorate at The University of Texas in Austin. While working on his doctorate he was a teaching assistant in the English Department at the University of Texas. He was also an adjunct instructor at Austin Community College for six years and taught English, Humanities, and Religious Studies. Completing all his course work, he decided to suspend work on his doctorate and write his first national best seller, **The Flying Boy: Healing the Wounded Man**, a memoir now in its 18th printing, has sold over 250,000 copies as well as the screen rights. **The Flying Boy II: The Journey Continues**, his second memoir, sold over 175,000 copies.

Lee has published 24 books in the fields of personal growth, Recovery, Men's Issues, Spritualty, Relationships, and Creativity. He has had two national bestsellers and his first novel, When the Buddha Met Bubba, penned under the pseudonym, Richard Dixie Hartwell, is soon to be released as a movie.

While Lee has a strong literary background, he is also a recognized leader in the fields of Recovery and Addiction, Men's Issues, Anger Management, Relationships, and has trained counselors and therapists nationally and internationally. He is the founder and former director of The Austin Men's Center established in Austin, Texas in 1986.

Over the past 30 years, Lee has consulted and trained prestigious institutions in the clinical environment: The Cleveland Clinic, The Betty Ford Clinic, Guy's Hospital (London, England), The New York Open Center, South Pacific Private Hospital (Sydney), and Mountain Area Health and Education Center (North Carolina), among others. He has keynoted over 300 major conferences on Recovery, Personal Growth, Men's Issues, and Relationships, and is considered a leading authority in the field of Anger Management. Currently Lee speaks in various cities and countries each year and works with clients in his unique intensive formats in Austin, Texas.

He has been featured on Dr. Oz, Oprah Winfrey, 20/20, Barbara Walter's The View, CNN, PBS, and NPR, and has been interviewed by Newsweek, Glamour Magazine, The New York Times, The Los Angeles Times, Austin American Statesman, and dozens of other national magazines and radio talk shows. His highly creative developments in anger management workshops, PEER™ Counseling seminars, mini-sessions, and the all-new Detour Method (lecture and workshop series on facing regression), are taught worldwide. Lee and poet Robert Bly taught over

20 seminars, conferences, and workshops around the country positioning him as one of the early pioneers in the Men's Movement.

OTHER BOOKS AND AUDIO PROGRAMS
BY JOHN LEE

Books

The Flying Boy Letters: Getting Back to Y'all 30 Years Later. Palm Desert: Robert Teitelbaum Publishing, 2019.

Breaking the Mother-Son Dynamic: Resetting the Patterns of a Man's Life and Loves. Deerfield Beach: Health Communications, Inc., 2015.

The Half-Lived Life: Overcoming Passivity and Rediscovering Your Authentic Self. Guildford: Lyons Press 2012.

Emotional Intelligence for Couples: Simple Ways to Increase the Communication in Your Relationship. Turner Publishing, 2011.

The Anger Solution: The Proven Method for Achieving Calm and Developing Healthy, Long-Lasting Relationships. Cambridge: Da Capo Press, 2009.

The Missing Peace: Solving the Anger Problem for Alcoholics/ Addicts and Those Who Love Them. Teitelbaum Publishing.

The Secret Place of Thunder: The Poetry & Prose of Knowing. Woodstock: Monarch Publishing Associates, 2004.

Courting a Woman's Soul: Going Deeper into Loving and Being Loved. Woodstock: Teitelbaum Publishing.

Growing Yourself Back Up: Understanding Emotional Regression. New York: Three Rivers Press, 2001.

The Dragon's Letters. Minneapolis: Ally Press, 1995.

Too Much Talk or Too Little. Pewaukee: Honey Creek Publishing, 1994.

Writing from The Body: For Writers, Artists, and Dreamers Who Long to Free Their Voice. New York: St. Martin's Press, 1994.

A Quiet Strength: Meditations on the Masculine Soul. New York: Bantam, 1994.

Facing The Fire: Experiencing and Expressing Anger Appropriately. New York: Bantam, 1992.

At My Father's Wedding. New York: Bantam, 1991. Hardcover Book of the Month Club and Quality Paperback Books. Has been translated into German, French and released in a U.K. version.

Recovery: Plain and Simple. Deerfield Beach: Health Communications, Inc., 1990.

The Flying Boy Book II: The Journey Continues. Teitelbaum Publishing.

The Flying Boy: Healing The Wounded Man. Deerfield Beach: Health Communications, Inc., 1987. Listed as a best seller by Publishers Weekly. The Flying Boy has been translated into Chinese, Japanese, Dutch, Greek and Spanish. Sold movie rights.

Audio

available at: https://www.creativechangeconferences.com/shop

The Flying Boy. Creative Change Conferences, 2021

How to Love Someone Without Losing Yourself. Creative Change Conferences, 2021

Why Men Can't Feel and The Price Women Pay. Creative Change Conferences, 2021

Saying Goodbye to Mom and Dad. Creative Change Conferences, 2021

When Buddha Met Bubba.

Anger vs. Rage.

Saying Good-bye to Mom and Dad. Boulder: Sounds True.

CONTACT INFORMATION

John Lee Books and Seminars
511 E 39th Street
Austin, TX 78751

Office 678-494-1296
Assistant: Kathy McClelland 334-332-3301

www.ingramcontent.com/pod-product-compliance
Lightning Source LLC
Chambersburg PA
CBHW060319030426
42336CB00011B/1121